Afterlife Mysteries Revealed

Afterlife Mysteries Revealed

By
Kalila Smith
with
Stephanie Link

Afterlife Mysteries Revealed

Copyright © 2013, 2016 Kalila Smith

Cover design by Lori Osif

All rights reserved. No part of this book may be reproduced, duplicated, copied, or transmitted in any form or by any means without the express written consent and permission of the author and publisher.

This is a work of memory and storytelling. The names, characters, places, and incidents are known publicly, are common knowledge, or are used only from a memoir point of view. All opinions and events related are told from the author's point of view.

Published by
Dark Oak Press
Kerlak Enterprises, Inc.
Memphis, TN
www.darkoakpress.com

Trade Paperback
ISBN 13: 978-1-937035-59-4
Library of Congress Control Number: 2013950766
First Printing: 2013
Second Printing: 2016

This book is printed on acid free paper.

Printed in the United States of America

Dedicated to my beloved daughter,
Stephanie Nicole (Kippy) Link,
March 1, 1983 – January 25, 2013

I think of you every minute of every day. You are in my thoughts, my dreams, and my heart always. Your memory lives on as long as I live and write. Without you, this book would not be possible. I miss you and love you.

Drawing of Stephanie Link by artist medium, Janette Kaye 6/21/13

Acknowledgments

My sincere thanks to everyone who shared their own experiences with ADCs and DBEs, stories of my daughter, and stood beside me during my darkest hours: Patricia Lund, Angela Shockley, Kathryn Morrow, Kim Schlosser Tuminello, Chastity Bowen, Amber, Megan, and Brittany Pearson, Nina De Santo, Sidney Smith, Hugh Palmer, Bobbi Lynn Harrigan, Tanya Vandesteeg, William Arendell, Allan Gilbreath, Anna Parmalee, Patti Levie, Patricia Lund, Denise Baudier, Heather Monell, and Phillip Humphries.

Many thanks to those who have walked down this road before me who contributed their stories, advice, inspiration, and wisdom: Terri Daniel, Christine Duminiak, Ara Parisien, Melena Landry, Janette Kay, Sid Patrick, Dr. Eben Alexander, Dr. Raymond Moody, and Dr. Jeffrey Long. I offer a huge thank you to everyone at Dark Oak Media and Press for their continued support and assistance.

A very special thank you to my angels, George, Gary, and Stephanie. Knowing you are still there for me keeps me going.

Table of Contents

Foreword by Dr. Jeffrey Long i
Preface 1
Introduction..5
Chapter 1 - How We Die 11
Chapter 2 - How We Grieve 19
Chapter 3 - Lost in a Fog 27
Chapter 4 - Hauntings..35
Chapter 5 - NDEs: Are They a Sign of an Afterlife? 47
Chapter 6 - ADCs: Real Experiences or Figments of Our
   Imaginations?..53
Chapter 7 - My Early Signs 59
Chapter 8 - Dreams...69
Chapter 9 - Remembering..77
Chapter 10 - Messages..87
Chapter 11 - Finally, Contact! 97
Chapter 12 - In Search of God 105
Chapter 13 - Angels..113
Chapter 14 - Watchers, Walkers, & Between World.......121
Chapter 15 - Visions of Heaven but What about Hell? ...127
Chapter 16 - Messages Continue 133
Chapter 17 - The Doctor, the Evidence, and the
   Verdict 139
Chapter 18 - The Afterlife Awareness Conference 149
Chapter 19 - Photographic Evidence 157
Chapter 20 - Deathbed Experiences 163
Chapter 21 - How the Mediums Work 173
Chapter 22 - Healing From Grief..................................181
Chapter 23 - Living Life in a New Way 189
Chapter 24 - Final Thoughts 197
Resources..201
Bibliography 203
About the Author 207

Foreword

As a radiation oncologist I have been trained to approach medicine very conservatively. In my work I must be very cautious with life and death situations. I approach the subject of the afterlife with the same cautiousness. I have spent many years researching and documenting thousands of near death experiences from all over the world. My organization, Near Death Experience Research Foundation (NDERF), has the largest collection of NDEs in the world. Our web site is offered in over twenty languages. Having documented NDEs from various people from every walk of life, from different cultures, and a multitude of religious paths, the evidence is so powerful that I can say with complete confidence that there is most definitely an afterlife.

In addition to my research with NDERF, I am a founder for the After Death Communication Research Foundation (ADCRF). This organization has documented thousands of cases of After Death Communications (ADC) from all over the world. ADC is a common and important experience which has received surprisingly little study. We define ADC as "A spontaneous experience of communication with a deceased friend or family member."

This definition encompasses experiences of communication from the deceased which are spontaneous. This definition excludes deceased entities encountered using mediums, psychics, hypnosis, or through channeling. We recognize communication can occur in these ways, and may be meaningful. What is clear is that ADC is <u>not</u> a hallucination nor is it a mental or psychiatric dysfunction. They are real. ADC experiencers we talked with generally felt their experience was significant and meaningful.

Kalila Smith with Stephanie Link

Several studies found that among parents of children who die, a very high percentage report an ADC within a few months of the child's death. We consider an ADC a gift. The gift of an ADC comforts our grief and reassures us that we will be reunited with our loved one at the time of our death and for all eternity. Even after reviewing over 2000 ADCs, what Kalila experienced from her daughter are among the most remarkable and evidential ADCs ever. I am delighted that she is writing this up for a book. The world needs to hear about this!

Jeffrey Long, M.D.

Preface

"The most beautiful people in the world are those who have known defeat, known suffering, known struggle, known loss, and have found their way out of the depths. These people have an appreciation, a sensitivity, and an understanding of life that fills them with compassion, gentleness, and a deep loving concern. Beautiful people do not just happen." ~ Elisabeth *Kübler-Ross*

This book is a product of my own experiences with death and grief. I have written numerous books on hauntings and paranormal experience, but never intended to delve this deeply into the world beyond the veil that separates our physical world from the one beyond. Death changed all that. When death came to my door and stole what was most precious to me, everything changed.

We all know that we, or someone we love will die, but few of us live our lives obsessing over when that might happen. It would neither be wise nor healthy to live in fear of death constantly. So we tuck away those fears deep in our subconscious mind; out of the way of our day to day thoughts. We wind up living as if we will live forever. Although I had certainly made proper arrangements in the event of my own demise, I did not waste my time lingering over the when's, the where's or the how's.

When death came to my household, it appeared as an unexpected, uninvited guest. It took my child without notice or preparation. I was left in a state of shock. My entire world was shattered. One minute, she was fine; the next, she was gone. Thus began a journey into the forbidden world of the dead. My past experiences had merely picked at the surface of what existed on the other side.

This book is an account of that journey. I candidly shared my experiences in an attempt to hopefully encourage others to embark on their own journey. We will all die someday or will lose someone we believe we cannot live without. This book is to help those who feel lost because it is happening to them. This book is for those who have wondered if there is life after death. It is also for those who fear death and hope that there is something beyond, but have not yet truly come to believe.

It is this author's intent to help heal those who grieve the loss of someone they loved. I wrote my own experiences straight from my heart. I have lost not only beloved family members and friends but one of my own children. I learned from my personal path through grief that the one thing that gave me comfort was the thought that my daughter continued beyond this world. During my darkest hours when I had lost all faith, I fell deep into the abyss of depression. Proof of an afterlife helped me and it can help others. This book is more than a book to prove that life continues after this one, many before me have already done that. It is to help give the bereaved comfort that their loved ones are somewhere else and that they will see them again. I shared the most intimate details of the most painful experience in my life in order to give hope to others. You never get over the loss of a loved one but you can learn to live with that loss. You can find your way to peace and remember the happy times rather than focus on the loss. No one can possibly understand what you are going through unless they have experienced it. This is especially true for parents who have lost a child. I know what loss is. I have lived through the pain.

The friends and family of those who hurt so deeply because of the death of a loved one might find useful insight for directing them on a path of healing. I also hope that therapists and counselors will find this book useful. Often those suffering from grief find it difficult to believe anything. The slightest sign that their loved one might be nearby can be a great comfort and facilitate healing.

Those who counsel the bereaved must be open-minded to the possibility that life does continue after this life. Even if you yourself do not necessarily believe, it is essential that you be empathetic to the needs and beliefs of your clients. Educating yourself on this subject can be very useful in your practice.

The messages herein are for those facing death and the caretakers who must assist them during their final days. When I was studying for my certifications in counseling and bodywork, I was required to do a certain amount of community service volunteer hours. I chose to do mine at Project Lazarus House, a hospice facility for advanced stage AIDS patients. For the people who lie in beds waiting for death to take them, it can be very frightening. They may have had months or even years knowing that they would face death soon. These brave individuals must embrace the inevitable whether they are ready or not.

This book is for all the skeptics who do not believe that there is life beyond this one. In Gestalt therapy, one of our favorite slogans is "get out of your head and come to your senses." There is much more than what meets the eye. Some things are beyond explanation. Sometimes there are things we feel, see, hear, taste, or smell that defy physical and logical explanation. Keep an open mind; expect the unexpected.

There will always be skeptics and it is not my intention to try to change someone's beliefs. I do wonder how many skeptics become fearful or worried when death does come to call. In those final hours, what are the thoughts of the skeptic or the atheist? Do they feel totally at ease believing that when they breathe their final breath that they will just disappear into nothingness?

And lastly, this book is for all who have experienced the other side. It is for those who think they might have experienced something and are not sure. This is your opportunity to push the envelope and explore what might be out there. For those who know they've experienced something and were too afraid to step forward because you feared no one would believe you; you are not alone. For the mediums who wish to learn more on what they are channeling, this book is for you too.

Kalila Smith with Stephanie Link

Right now, someone is taking their last breath, preparing to cross over to the next realm of reality. Right now, someone is sitting at the bedside of loved one, watching them die. Right now, someone is lying in a hospital bed, awakening from a near death experience and no one believes what they are describing. Right now, a parent is facing a sudden death of a beloved child and that person's heart is breaking in half. Right now is the time for us to open our minds to the possibility of an afterlife and an entirely different approach of dealing with death.

Life is not something we should take for granted. There is a purpose for all of us. Death is a part of life, we cannot avoid it. Our society has become one that treats death as taboo, refusing to accept it. The more we understand about it, the less we have to fear.

Introduction

"They that love beyond the world cannot be separated by it. Death cannot kill what never dies." ~ Williams Penn

Nothing lasts forever. I had learned the hard way that nothing in life was permanent or guaranteed. In the blink of an eye, everything can change. By the end of 2012, I had gained and lost numerous jobs, husbands, and fortunes several times over. Living in South Louisiana and having survived natural disasters such as hurricane Katrina taught me that in at any given moment, all sense of security can be ripped away. Security was only an illusion. Disasters strike, divorce happens, and jobs run their course.

I lived about thirty miles outside of New Orleans with my developmentally disabled daughter, Stephanie, and our pets. Life wasn't perfect but it was happy and peaceful. Every day I strived to do something productive and to be happy with who I was and what I had. What I was not prepared for was her death. Nothing can ever prepare a parent for the loss of a child. In January, 2013, my life changed forever when she died, suddenly.

Stephanie had lived her entire life with me. Because she was mentally handicapped, she never moved out to live on her own. She was always much like a younger child. She enjoyed spending weekends either home with me or accompanying me on travel adventures when the opportunity presented itself. She followed me on film shoots, convention appearances, and the occasional tour. She was my little side-kick, or as she liked to call herself, my mascot.

Kalila Smith with Stephanie Link

Stephanie had always been in good health for a Down syndrome person. She had some weird infections from time to time but nothing life threatening. In the winter of 2012, she developed an upper respiratory infection that caused her tonsils to inflame and swell. The doctor noted that her tonsils were so swollen that they were practically touching. We were sent to a specialist for a second opinion.

The ENT specialist agreed that it would be necessary to remove her tonsils as soon as possible. We arranged for her surgery to take place the following month, after the holidays. We went about our business celebrating Christmas and New Year's as usual. Then in January we began the preparation for her surgery.

On January 23, 2013, Stephanie was admitted to the hospital for what should have been a routine outpatient surgical procedure. She sailed through the procedure with no problems. Of course she was tired and in pain when she came out of recovery but was alert and able to communicate her needs. I took photos of her in her hospital bed with her teddy dressed in scrubs to accompany her to surgery. She was released the following day after being examined, showing no signs of complications or infection. When she was released she had no fever, no coughing, and was alert. I brought Stephanie home where she slept on and off, waking up periodically to go to the bathroom and drink juice and water.

The following morning she awakened at about 9:00 AM crying in pain. She had slept for nine hours without pain medication, so of course she felt pain at that point. I gave her medication which included an antibiotic that was prescribed in the hospital two days before to ward off infection. She went back to sleep after eating a light meal and sipping on a fruit smoothie. At 2:30 PM her caretaker, Nicole, arrived to relieve me so I could go to work. I didn't leave right away, but rather continued to do as I had been that morning, setting up the guest room.

At around 4:30 PM Nicole walked Stephanie to the bathroom. Afterwards she crawled back in her bed and took a few sips of smoothie and some water. She then went back to sleep. In less than a half hour Nicole called me into Stephanie's room saying she "didn't look right." I saw her lying there with bubbles and saliva coming out of her mouth. She was still breathing the same rhythmic breath that she did when sleeping soundly. I grabbed her arm to pull her up but she was limp. I felt her shoulder pull a bit at the socket. This frightened me that I would hurt her so I set her arm back on the bed. I was in total shock. I called out to her again and again, but she was nonresponsive. I opened her eyes and saw that her pupils were very small. I stood over her in shock, speechless. I couldn't move. I could barely breathe. I was frozen with shock.

"Call 911," Nicole instructed.

The wait seemed forever. She continued to breathe but did not respond to my voice. I felt helpless. I paced back and forth nervously until the EMT unit arrived, forcing me to leave the room. They worked on her for at least a half hour. I stood outside crying and praying that they could help her. I begged God not to keep her. Something deep inside of me told me that although she breathed, she was not in that body.

"Send her back, I know you can send her back, she's still breathing, it's not too late," I prayed.

With my head spinning, I called friends and family, reaching out to whomever I could in desperation to aid me in this helpless state I was in. I felt a sinking feeling in my chest. I wanted to run, I wanted to punch the brick wall of my garage, and I wanted to avoid this; to wake up from this nightmare. A large part of me died that night with her. I could not imagine my life without her. Immediately I felt like I was half out of my body. I sat in shock as the coroner went to her room and did whatever it was he did. I watched as my child's body was brought out in a black zipped bag. The coroner walked over to me solemnly and said in his Cajun accent, "Sorry for your loss, cher."

All I can remember is barely being able to utter a word at that time. My world became dark and dismal. I wanted to die myself. I remember vaguely only being able to take short, shallow breaths. I felt as if I was going to suffocate. My mind was jumbled and I could not string a concise thought together, much less a sentence.

I became crippled with grief. Most days, I was plagued with sudden panic attacks and uncontrollable crying. Even though Stephanie was an adult in age, she was still a child mentally. She was my "forever" child. I had spent almost thirty years caring for her. Every decision in my life revolved around her. She was my reason for existing. She had been my life. Most resources agreed that to lose a child at any age was the most profound type of grief known. But to lose someone like Stephanie was even more difficult. The attachment between the mother and a child with special needs is different from normal bonds.

Having spent the past almost twenty years of my life writing about spirit communication, I expected immediate signs from her. In hindsight, I did get quite a few very significant signs in the very beginning, but I was so grief-stricken and still in shock that most of the signs overwhelmed or frightened me. Then I second-guessed myself, wondering if I had experienced what I did because it was what I wanted to believe. My world became a living hell. I later came to understand that grief was to blame. No one can understand how grief takes hold until it happens to them.

Once the dust settled and the funeral was over and everyone else went back to their own lives, I wanted more signs but got nothing. All I felt was the searing pain of loss. What I wanted was not possible. I wanted my daughter back. Every day was a nightmare. The emptiness I felt every morning was unbearable. Most nights I would cry for a while in my driveway before I could even bring myself to go inside. I desperately wanted signs to comfort me that she was still somewhere and that it was a good place.

In the following weeks, I was in a fog. My heart literally ached for her. I felt as if my very soul had been pulled apart. A piece of me was missing. My every thought was on her. Where did she go? Why was she taken from me? I played the last few moments of her life over and over again in my head. What did I do wrong? Why was God punishing me so? I felt robbed. My beautiful daughter was gone forever from my life, and I could barely breathe. I was stuck in a state of panic.

I called the surgeon who was equally perplexed at her unexpected death. He and I went over each minute of the last two days of her life. At the end of it all, we both agreed that neither of us could have done anything differently that would have created a different outcome. No one saw this coming. No one could have predicted nor prevented it. She had no symptoms and was on antibiotics for two days.

My belief that all things work for the best for all concerned no longer applied. I no longer believed that God never gave a person anything that they cannot handle. In fact, I hardly even believed in God at all at this point. How could I? My daughter was ripped from my life without warning! In the throngs of grief I was overcome with emotions. It seemed that with Stephanie's passing, all bets were off. I believed nothing that I had before. Everything I had researched, written about, or thought I knew went out the window; as did all logic.

"She was recovering remarkably well then, with no warning, she died in her sleep. It didn't make sense. It wasn't fair," I lamented.

For the first few months following her death, I desperately sought out anything and everything to confirm that she was still somewhere and that she was okay. The thought of my daughter just disappearing into nonexistence drove me insane. It challenged every belief I ever had. I became so confused that I was no longer sure what I believed anymore, if anything at all.

I read numerous books on grief in the hopes of working through my misery. I came upon a section on one web site that said a symptom of grief included seeing, hearing or smelling the departed loved one, but that it merely represented a *harmless memory*. The thought that my experiences were nothing more than memories drove me to madness.

"I just imagined this?" I screamed inside myself, "None of it was real? The signs I've seen my entire life were nothing more than fantasies? If that is the case, then where is Stephanie?"

I became obsessed with probing further into proving the existence of an afterlife. I had spent so many years investigating paranormal activity but dealt with hauntings left on the physical plane. It had already been determined that over ninety percent of all hauntings were not an intelligent spirit but an energetic impression; a residual haunting.

"What if," I wondered, "all hauntings were simply residual energy? What if there *is* nothing else beyond this world? What if I've made all of this up, convincing myself of nothing more than fairy tales?"

I began peering beyond the veil that separated our world and whatever there was on the other side. I was so disillusioned that I was not sure anything even existed at all beyond this world. I hoped that I could prove myself wrong. I became my own worst skeptic. But I would examine all of the evidence and try to sort out what was real and what was not. I hoped to find answers and some solace that my daughter who had been my entire world was still somewhere and that I would see her again.

Chapter One
How We Die

"Watching a peaceful death of a human being reminds us of a falling star; one of a million lights in a vast sky that flares up for a brief moment only to disappear into the endless night forever."
~ Dr. Elisabeth Kubler-Ross

Death has many faces. Some people die by accident. Many people die in automobile accidents, plane or train accidents, accidental drowning, accidents involving weapons, or accidents that are caused by medications. Some die at the hands of others. Others die in wars or natural disasters. Most of us hope, some even assume, that when our time comes it will be peacefully in our sleep; at old age, after a long and happy life has been fulfilled. But for many people, death can be a lingering process.

Sometimes slow death from illness happens earlier in life. Not all who die from cancer or other diseases are geriatrics. But because we cannot predict accidents, murders, or other causes of sudden death we will examine death that comes upon us slowly; taking its time.

When this type of death occurs, there are many dynamics at work, both involving the person who is dying as well as family, friends, and caretakers involved in the process. This is an extremely difficult set of circumstances. On the one hand, it gives the dying person a chance to make final arrangements and say good-bye to friends and family. But it also makes way for the fears associated with death to be addressed directly. This can be a very frightening time for the dying person, as well as those who are close to them. None of us wish for our loved ones to suffer, but at the same time, none of us want them to die either.

Grief comes early for those waiting for a loved one to die an expected death. This type of grief is *anticipatory grief* and it is very complicated. The dying person also experiences grief that follows the same steps as with any other type of grieving. Everyone involved begins grieving the moment the individual learns that they are dying. The first step is always *denial*.

Several months after my daughter died, a very close friend learned that she had stage-four cancer. I had known this woman for almost thirty years. She had been so close to my family it was as if she was family.

She had undergone several other bouts with cancer, ranging from minor skin cancers, from over exposure to sun in her younger days and later, colon cancer. She always seemed to recover and move on to her active life. This time it seemed that cancer had won. She was older now, in her seventies, and the cancer had now metastasized into her lungs and bloodstream. This woman loved life and had always been very active. The last thing she was ready for was death. She had been a devout Christian yet the thought of dying terrified her. Even after doctors informed her that she had no hope for recovering this time, she remained hopeful that she might have more time than she actually did.

When I first saw her not long after she learned of the severity of illness, she said to me, "Let's go out and have dinner sometime. I know you probably aren't up to it yet, but in a few months, maybe."

I was so shocked I did not know how to respond. I just agreed for the moment and later called my sister-in-law and asked if this woman was aware of her condition. She was barely able to walk due to pain from the tumors throughout her body.

"How could she think that she would possibly be able to go out in a few months?" I wondered to myself.

Because she was in *denial*, she acted as if she did not know that she was going to die. She did not want to believe that this time she was not going to recover. Her children too, faced with anticipatory grief were in denial as well. Her daughter continued to bring her to doctors in hopes of treating the cancer. They were both crushed when one oncologist finally said to them, "There is nothing more that we can do."

Within a week, she was in the hospital with her family again hoping for a cure. This time she was sent home and the family arranged for hospice. I visited her once she was settled into her son's home. Her daughter mentioned that she was being contrary and difficult. She was emerging into the next stage, *anger*.

The second emotional stage of grief is anger. Most people get angry at doctors during this stage. Why would the doctor say such a thing? Why aren't they trying harder to get the person well? They can be angry at medical staff, family members for not understanding, or at themselves. Usually while the person is still alive, anger will not be directed so much at God. In fact, most people will become more spiritual or religious when facing death. This becomes useful in the following stage which is bargaining.

The one who is facing death, as well as loved ones, often bargain with God for a cure or at least more time. It is very common for those who have faith to turn to prayer during a crisis. Some sources are much more scientific or medical and seem to view this as just another stage. For those who do have faith, it is a way to seek comfort. Personally, I do not like using the word *bargaining,* even though it is considered part of the normal pattern for any grieving process. I consider moving forward on a spiritual path or asking for Divine intervention or comfort to be beneficial to the dying individual and their family. It is crucial for those facing death to find comfort at this point. Aligning oneself spiritually is extremely important. It is also an opportunity for spiritual growth for those who are involved with the dying.

The next stage is depression and along with it, regret. The dying person may reflect on their life and wish they had done things differently. Some become sad because now it is too late. There is never enough time in life. Regardless of age, the dying person will always wish that they had more time. Depression is very hard on the body physically. It makes an already sick person, even weaker. Even in a healthy body, depression weakens the immune system. For the critically ill, depression can escalate pain and the progression of the illness. It is during this time, if one has not done so earlier, to offer counseling to the dying and the family to help cope. It is also important at this time that friends and family offer love and support to the dying person helping them move on to the final stage, which is acceptance.

Once acceptance is achieved then the person can make their final arrangements and spend quality time with loved ones. It is important to let that person know that their life was meaningful and had positive impacts on others. Nothing is taken for granted at this stage. It is the final stage in which the person can enjoy what life has left to offer. This is an important time for the dying to see loved ones, enjoy a day out if possible, or take part in what they enjoy one last time.

It is important to respect the wishes of the person who is dying. Try to make their last bits of time here as comfortable as possible. Allow the person to share stories from their life experiences. Sometimes the person will want to reconnect with people they have not seen in a long time. If at all possible, help find them and make that contact.

Everybody dies differently, but there are certain things that are common in the final stages of life for the terminally ill. The first stage is withdrawal from life. There is a loss of interest in activities that were once considered pleasurable. The individual also begins to sleep more. They lose interest in living, becoming detached from the physical world.

Although she was not terminally ill, my daughter had become less interested in life in the last months of her life. Even though she actually died from a very obscure infection, she suffered from early onset Alzheimer's disease. For the last year and a half of her life, she had lost interest in many of the activities she had once loved.

Only in recent years have these individuals lived long enough for doctors to realize the connection between Alzheimer's disease and Down syndrome. Most of them had full blown Alzheimer's disease before the age of forty. The gene for Alzheimer's disease is located on the twenty-first chromosome, and in Down syndrome, there was an extra twenty-first chromosome. That meant that these people got an extra dose of the gene that causes Alzheimer's disease. Some of them displayed symptoms of the dementia associated with Alzheimer's in their early twenties. Unfortunately, such was the case with my daughter.

Over time, Alzheimer's disease causes a death to nerve cells in the brain. Brain tissue deteriorates leading to memory loss and loss of skills. The cortex literally shrinks and dead spaces of the brain fill with fluid. The dead nerve cells become tangled strands of proteins. In persons with Down syndrome, these tangles can be present as early as the second decade of life.

Unlike normal individuals who develop Alzheimer's disease in later life, persons with Down syndrome do not display the memory issues that older individuals do. To the untrained eye, the disease goes almost unnoticed. What happens more frequently in Down syndrome is that they decline in cognition and become less cooperative. Stephanie had always loved her job, swimming, video games, and movies. As time went on, she enjoyed these things less and less. She became obsessed with late night television shows from her early childhood. She refused to go to bed, staying up late to watch these shows then refusing to get up in the morning for her job. Alzheimer's is often called a living death. The body continues to live but the personality dies, little by little.

Another sign of impending death in terminally ill patients is experiencing visions of another world or visits from deceased loved ones. Many professionals write this off as possible hallucinations, but quite a few believe that these people are actually seeing what is to come in the next level of existence for them. Deathbed visions and experiences will be explored at greater length in another chapter. It is important to remember that when these experiences are described by the dying individual; do not judge or dismiss what is being experienced. These visions serve to comfort the dying person and can be of comfort to the family as well.

As the body dies, the organs began to shut down. This is completely normal as everything does not just die all at once. It is a process. Because of this, one of the first signals that death is soon is the patient loses interest in food. This can be very disturbing to family members but it is important not to force food or liquids which can be a source of choking for the individual. Because food and water intake are decreased, urine and bowel movement changes are to be expected.

Additional signs include restlessness and confusion which are often caused by metabolic changes and a decrease in oxygen. Breathing is also affected. Breaths can be shallow and slow or rapid and intense. Cheyne-Stokes breathing is a common sign that death is near indicated by deep, frequent breaths followed by periods of no breath at all for up to forty-five seconds. Gurgles in the throat giving way to the *death rattle* can be alarming to family members. Secretions in the back of the throat build up and the cough reflex is no longer working, causing this gurgling sound. A sudden high fever can also be a sign of death approaching. This is usually followed by the temperature dropping dramatically. Skin is cool and damp to the touch.

As death approaches, it is important that the individual is given permission to die by loved ones. Some people will actually linger as they wait for particular loved ones to be near or say good-bye. I discovered after my daughter had passed away that children often will die when their parents are not there because it is too difficult to do so with the parents present. When my brother passed away, his wife was upstairs. Only his daughter was present. As he struggled to breathe, she told him, "It's okay, Daddy, you can let go."

He then took his last breath.

Many people will wait for certain people to leave the room for them to move on. I believe my brother waited for his wife to leave the room. On a couple of occasions, she thought he was dying and got hysterical, grabbing him and screaming his name. I do not think it was coincidental that he died when she was in another room.

It is equally important for the dying person to say good-bye as it is for those left behind. One of the complications of grief can occur when sudden death is to blame and no one gets to say good-bye. It is also important that the dying person knows that their responsibilities are taken care of, their loved ones will survive, they are forgiven, and that they will be remembered. These are all very important issues for closure for both sides. It is always important to remember that even if the dying person is unconscious, they may still hear and understand what is being said. Hearing is the last sense to die. Loved ones and caretakers must never assume that the person cannot hear them.

Lastly, any religious rites or rituals should be performed during this time.

Even when the death is expected and loved ones experience anticipatory grief, once death has occurred grieving will continue and be more intense.

One of the most profound examples of proof of life existing beyond physical death is sometimes witnessed by those present at the time of death. Some claim to have actually seen the soul leaving the physical body. When I was training in bodywork and energy healing, one of my instructors had done extensive work with the dying. She told me that when some of her clients died, she was with them. She had witnessed a white puff of what looked like smoke or a mist exiting from the crown chakra area at the top of the skull. Throughout time, others have claimed to see the same thing. This is the first bit of evidence in favor of an existence beyond the physical body. If we see the spirit exiting, where does it go?

Chapter Two
How We Grieve

"There is a sacredness in tears. They are not the mark of weakness, but of power. They speak more eloquently than ten thousand tongues. They are the messengers of overwhelming grief, of deep contrition, and of unspeakable love." ~ Washington Irving

Everybody grieves differently. There is no right or wrong way to grieve. There is no timetable for grieving. But there are specific stages that take place when a loved one dies. The stages are identical to other forms of grieving such as anticipatory grief when we learn the loved one is dying. These stages are common in any type of loss. The degree to which we experience the stages depends on the loss. Usually grief is directly proportional to the love that is lost. The greater the love, the more pain we feel when we grieve that loss. Grief has often been referred to as the price we pay for loving so intensely. It is a very personal experience.

Having raised a disabled child, I was no stranger to grief. My grief began when I learned of my child's disability. She was born on March 1, 1983 in Charlotte, North Carolina. It had been a particularly difficult pregnancy. I was forced to spend most of my time off of my feet to prevent any mishaps. Remarkably, I made it through full term. On one of my doctor visits, it was determined that the baby would be about seven pounds. But something happened once she had turned. Two weeks after the doctor announced her estimated weight, he remarked that the baby was not as big as he had thought. At that time, the ultrasound was something that was done once, and it was performed in the hospital not routinely in the doctor's office. So he did not order another one. Two weeks later, I went into labor.

Once I checked into the hospital I was placed in a small labor room and was hooked up to monitors. It was 1983 so there was no elaborate digital equipment. Every time I had a contraction, the baby's heart rate practically stopped. The nurse moved the machine a bit and reset it. She checked the connections. She seemed to be more concerned with the equipment being faulty rather than there might be something wrong with my baby. When my baby's heart rate dropped for the third time, she brought in a different machine. The doctor walked in as she fidgeted with the second one and ordered her to prep me for immediate surgery. I was rolled into the delivery room screaming for my baby.

When I woke up hours later, I was told that I had a girl. When I asked to see her the nurse informed me that she was on another floor in neonatal intensive care being treated as a *preemie*. I was still groggy from the anesthesia but I knew something was dreadfully wrong. My baby was not premature but full term. I later learned that her cord had twisted just enough when she turned that it cut off her nutrients causing her to lose weight. Although she was eighteen inches long she only weighed five pounds, seven ounces.

Once I was fully awake, I was wheeled to the neonatal intensive care unit to visit my baby. Her frail, thin, little body was curled up in an incubator. She had a mask over her eyes to protect from the ultraviolet lights that shone on her for jaundice. I put my hand through the opening in the incubator and laid it on her.

"It's going to be alright, Stephanie, Mommy's here," I whispered to her.

For the next ten days, the nurses wheeled me to see and feed her several times a day. My doctor lied on my medical record, claiming that I was bleeding so I was would not be discharged without my baby. During this time, the doctor introduced me to the neonatologist who informed me that she was doing chromosome tests on Stephanie. She felt Stephanie might have

Down syndrome. I had to wait days for the test results. I sat for hours in the rocking chair beside her incubator praying; begging God to let it be a mistake. I knew very little about Down syndrome other than it was something that happened with older mothers. I was only twenty-four at the time. I remained hopeful that it was all just a mistake. It wasn't. I was in shock and denial at this point.

Trisomy 21 Down syndrome is genetic disorder characterized by the presence of a third twenty first chromosome. People with Down syndrome suffer from a variety of physical abnormalities as well as moderate developmental delays. I was told that my daughter would be mentally retarded. The doctors further informed me that her life expectancy might be only into her mid-twenties. Although Stephanie showed the typical Down syndrome facial features, the flatter face, small eyes and nose, she did not suffer from some of the other physical effects of the syndrome. Many DS children are born with severe congenital heart and/or digestive track defects. Fortunately, she did not have any of these.

I challenged doctors and nurses. How could this be? I was only twenty-four! This was something that happened to women who got pregnant in their forties. It wasn't fair. One of the nurses brought me to the nursery and held a "normal" newborn lying across her hand. Even though the baby was only several hours old, it instinctively balanced itself on her hand, arching its little back and attempting to hold up its head. She later did the same with my baby. My little Stephanie hung over her hand like a limp dish rag. She had very little muscle tone at all.

When Stephanie was ten days old the diagnosis of Down syndrome had been confirmed. Although I immediately accepted my newborn regardless of her diagnosis, I still went through a period of grief. I had grieved before over the miscarriages I had suffered through. I was all too familiar with the process. I knew what it meant to grieve for what could have, should have been.

Grieving becomes accelerated when it is over the loss of what could have been because there is so much else to do with what *is*. The doctors had informed me that early intervention was the key to Stephanie's development. The more stimulation I could provide and the earlier I did it, the more she would learn. I wanted to give her the best shot at life that I could. Her early intervention program began at only two months of age.

This type of grief can be put on hold for many years. Because the sick family member is still alive, there is always hope for recovery. Family members generally do not get too caught up in the grief process as it would be too detrimental to the well-being of the sick family member. It is because we hope that we can make our child's life better that we are able to recover quickly from the grief associated with learning that our child has a disability. The time that we get to *fix it* varies depending on the child and the disability.

I fell into grief again a year and a half before my daughter died, when the doctor informed me that she had early onset Alzheimer's disease. But I got stuck in denial.

I made excuses for her and blamed workers even when she began to display very strange behavior. She cared less and less about her hygiene. She had always been very meticulous about it but had begun to not care. She insisted on wearing the same nightgown night after night. I had to sneak to wash it. One evening, she got hair remover from under the sink and put it on her scalp causing a bald spot. She did this then was horrified that she did it. When I asked her why she did it, she said she didn't know. I didn't realize that this was a symptom of the Alzheimer's rearing its hideous head.

The further she slipped into early onset dementia the more I slipped into denial. Once again, grief had taken hold of my life. I vacillated between denial and anger. Again, I was angry with God. As if Down syndrome was not enough, now I had to watch my already disabled child becoming even more disabled. What little bit of functioning brain she had would now become less functioning.

I didn't know it at the time but Alzheimer's had affected her ability to walk. It was after her death that I learned that the disease affected the gait. The balance issues she had were attributed to the brain disease. I had gotten special orthopedic shoes, lifts, and braces for her ankles to help stabilize her. She used a walker and sometimes a wheelchair, if we were going to be in a situation that required a lot of walking or standing. She could barely walk a half of a block without having to stop and rest her legs.

The other symptom I was unaware of at the time was something called *sun-downing*. Stephanie literally had her days and nights mixed up. She wanted to sleep all day and stay up all night. She was always a night owl, even as an infant but this had become much more pronounced. I often awakened in the middle of the night to find her sitting at the kitchen table coloring.

The different stages of grief are unpredictable. I remained in denial until Stephanie died unexpectedly and full-blown grief hit me like a freight train. It was only after her death that I was able to look back and see that she had been declining all along. Had she not been taken by this mystery infection that struck so suddenly, she would have slowly deteriorated with the *living death* of Alzheimer's disease.

It was shortly after Stephanie's death that my sister, twenty-two years my senior, was forced to move into a full-time nursing home. She had lived with her daughter, my niece, for over twenty years and now at the age of seventy-eight was unable to be left alone. She had severe diabetes and high blood pressure and suffered from a form of dementia caused by not taking her medication properly. Two days before my daughter's funeral, my sister had fallen and broken her hip. After surgery she spent a couple of weeks in rehab then was sent home.

She was not home twenty-four hours when she fell again. It became apparent that she would need around the clock supervision and was admitted to a nursing home. She grieved the loss of the life she knew and had grown accustomed to for so many years. At first, she denied the necessity of being supervised so strictly. Within a few days, anger set in and she resisted everything that was made available to help her. But in a few weeks, she accepted her new life in the facility. Her grief was very short-lived but it proved that grief was involved nonetheless. As long as life continues, there is hope for better conditions so grief is present but not as deep as when a death occurs.

We grieve so deeply over the death of a loved one because death is final. We grieve because we feel we will never see that person again. When a person loses a child, that pain is amplified. One of the most disturbing and painful parts for me was the thought that my child was gone forever and I would never see her again. The thought of my child no longer existing anywhere and no hope of ever seeing her again troubled me. The pain became unbearable.

When a loved one dies, we mourn their loss and go through the various stages of grief. We can go back and forth between stages time and time again. Renowned grief expert, Elisabeth Kubler-Ross was the first to determine the various stages of grief. The first being shock. No matter how prepared we are for a loss, shock in unavoidable. Along with it comes denial. When hit with any kind of loss when it involves your child, the first response is "I can't believe it," or "maybe it's a mistake."

During this stage, we attempt to answer unanswered questions. We also search for other explanations that might make the unpleasant news untrue. When we are grieving during the child's life, we are not allowed to stay in this particular stage very long. Our child needs us facing reality. If we stayed in denial or shock for any length of time, our child would suffer, fail to thrive, or possibly die. Maternal instinct is not going to allow that. During denial we are limited on what information we assimilate. We could not survive if all information hit our systems at one time. So during shock and denial, we are allowed to gradually take in the loss one bit at a time.

I was extremely disconnected and overwhelmed in this stage of my grief. Nothing seemed real. I felt as if I had an endless gaping wound in my chest. I could not imagine going on at that time. I literally survived one minute at a time. I had a very hard time understanding the simplest things during this time. My brain found it difficult to make sense of things going on around me.

For those who lose someone after a long illness, the grief is often accompanied by guilt. Often those who mourn feel a sense of relief that the suffering is over. This can create a tremendous amount of guilt. Sometimes the guilt makes no sense. Parents of children who have died unexpectedly often blame themselves for not protecting the child from death. We go over events leading to the death in an attempt to see if something could have been done differently to create a different outcome. Even though my daughter died of an infection that was asymptomatic, I still sifted over the final days of her life to see if someone was at fault for her illness going unnoticed. The fact of the matter was that no one could have predicted, nor changed, what happened. I had to accept this.

In the anger stage, it is easy to let feelings consume us. It is easy to become bitter. One of the most difficult things to do when you have a child that is disabled is to watch other children who are growing and developing normally while your child is not. We may become angry with doctors or medical staff, we may lash out at our partners or other family members, but most commonly the grieving parent becomes angry with God. It is common at this stage to blame God for the child's condition. For many years, I felt very angry with God for Stephanie's disability. Through the years I had a huge disconnection with anything spiritual because I felt cheated by God. I blamed God for *making* my child disabled.

Through studying Gestalt, a form of experiential therapy, I learned that anger is grief turned inside out. Usually during any kind of grieving process, we first externalize our anger. We become angry at everyone and everything we can, whether it makes sense or not. Most people blame those around them. They blame the doctors. They blame family and friends. And when they run out of people to blame, they hold God responsible.

Anger must be expressed rather than repressed. Holding anger in is extremely damaging to us mentally and physically. To disburse anger and work through is the beginning of healing. Anger can appear and reappear throughout our grieving process.

Usually when we stop being angry at those around us, we begin to internalize the anger and we are now angry with ourselves.

Even when we are finally in the last stage of grief, acceptance, we can always find ourselves starting the cycle over again. Greif comes in waves. Sometimes I thought I was holding it together and suddenly would be overcome with a crying spell that hit out of nowhere. It is very unpredictable and uncontrollable. I never knew when I would become inconsolable.

Grief never goes away. We never really get closure. A good way to work through grief is to talk it out with an understanding friend, other bereaved parents, or a grief counselor. Being able to talk about your feelings rather than holding everything in is best. Feeling safe is important. Best outlets for a safe place to express your emotions are with a qualified grief therapist and/or a grief support group. Being in the presence of a person or people who understand how you feel is important. No one knows what you are feeling except someone who has experienced it. One can stay in any one or more stages, or go back and forth for months, even years. In the case of the loss of a child, grieving begins when the child dies and continues throughout the life of the parent. One never gets over it, but rather learns to live with it.

Chapter Three
Lost in a Fog

"When the time comes for you to die, you need not be afraid, because death cannot separate you from God's love." ~ Charles H. Spurgeon

Grief creates a fog. It is a roller coaster ride of emotions that jerks you from one overreaction to another. In the grips of severe grief, life becomes dreamlike. After my daughter died, I was no longer certain of anything, other than that I was lost without her. No matter what the circumstances are surrounding the death of a child, no parent is prepared to face the finality of saying goodbye. In many cases, there will be anticipatory grief. The child becomes ill and death is expected. Most of us convince ourselves that we will be ready for the loss when it occurs. But we are not ever.

My daughter's death was sudden and unexpected, so on top of the usual grief, I suffered afterwards with post-traumatic stress disorder (PTSD). When I saw my daughter lying in that bed not moving, I froze. I called 911 but barely remember any details of the evening. When the medics came out and confirmed that she had died, I felt like someone had kicked me in my stomach and pulled out a piece of my heart at the same time. I wanted to scream but could do nothing but gasp for air. In a flash, she was gone from my life and I stood there feeling as if the life was draining out of me. Things immediately felt surreal. I could not get the image of her lying in bed unresponsive, and then carried out of my home in a body bag, out of my head. Nor could I shake the image of her lifeless body lying in the coffin. At the time, it seemed like a bad dream.

Kalila Smith with Stephanie Link

I seemed to have gone into a never ending panic attack at that point. I felt completely out of control. I was incapable of accomplishing even the slightest tasks. I kept going over what happened in my head again and again. I could not handle the intense feeling of loss that engulfed me. I felt numb one minute then without notice sobbed uncontrollably. No one understood. I had absolutely no control over my emotions. The loss was more than something in my conscious mind. This pain drove deep inside of me. A bond between me and my child had been severed.

Having trained many years before as a therapist, I was programmed to immediately try to find some balance. I bought numerous books of grief. I went to grief groups through the Compassionate Friends. I entered into private therapy. As part of my therapy, I wrote a book on grief; *Farewell, My Forever Child,* a tribute to my daughter and a tool to help other parents of special needs children. In my own search for help, I noticed that there were no books written specifically for special needs situations and very little even mentioned in the books that were available. Changing that was cathartic for me and gave me something to give to others to help them. Sometimes the best way to help ourselves is to help others. I knew Stephanie would want to help others as well. She had always been a very selfless person always caring for others.

While in the early stages of grief, it is normal to feel disconnected from reality. Physical symptoms can include feeling faint, lightheadedness, panic stricken, racing heart, and heaviness in the limbs. Many major details can easily be forgotten during this period of grief. During the first few weeks, I can best describe what I felt as being in a fog. My heart literally ached. I cried myself to sleep every night and awakened only to cry again. My every thought was on her. Where did she go? Why was she taken from me?

In the beginning phases of my grief, I seemed to have boundless energy. My body pumped massive amounts of epinephrine and norepinephrine, the fight or flight hormones. Many responses in the body come from encoding in our DNA.

According to many experts, when someone close to us dies, it triggers primal fears that we too may not survive. Our bodies respond as if we were in actual danger. Although I completely understand this school of thought, I do not completely agree with it. As with the term *bargaining* I believe it is a bit too scientific of an outlook totally dismissing the spiritual and emotional side of the loss. When we lose someone we are connected to, we feel as if we lose a part of ourselves. I do agree that our bodies produce the same hormones if we are in mortal danger but it could be said that we want to react with fight or flight with the truth we are facing. We either want to reject it, or run from it. It is important to recognize that the body produces the same reaction in grief that it does in stress and pain.

In those early days I could not keep still. I was on the go every second of each day until I dropped from exhaustion in the evenings. I stayed away from home as much as possible. I distracted myself with work, friends, and family as much as I could; anything to keep from facing going home to an empty house. I gave little thought to the physical effects of my grief. The hormones I produced raised my blood pressure and heart rate. They also depleted my serotonin giving way to depression and triggering emotional eating.

It was during the early phase of grief that my physical health began to take a nose dive. I had gained over twenty pounds due to emotional overeating in just two months. I constantly felt wired. I suffered from headaches and frequent onsets of panic attacks. I experienced chest pains, shortness of breath, body aches, restlessness, insomnia, and palpitations (heart racing). It is not uncommon to become physically sick as if you have the flu. Body aches and lethargy are common during this time.

I dragged myself to see the doctor. He discovered that my blood pressure was unusually high. He decided to prescribe beta blockers for me to reduce my blood pressure and "prevent me from having a heart attack." He also prescribed Prozac for depression. After two days of feeling worse than I've ever felt in my life, I ditched the Prozac. Anti-depressants are fine for people who need them; as in people who are clinically depressed.

Kalila Smith with Stephanie Link

I am not a fan of them for circumstantial depression. Of course a bereaved parent is going to feel sad. Muffling that normal reaction to the loss of a child will only serve to prolong the grief process. I experienced some hideous physical side effects on this medication and decided to face my grief head on.

Because I had never experienced high blood pressure before losing my child, I opted to get a second opinion from a heart specialist. Stress can cause a heart attack in a bereaved parent even if there had never been a previous heart condition. Since I was over fifty, I felt it could be a reality. The last thing that I needed was to rack up my own hospital expenses for a condition that could be controlled if caught in advance. This was a wake-up call for me. I had to take better care of myself. As much as I grieved for my lost child, I did not want to add the additional trauma to my other daughter and granddaughters by neglecting my own health.

Despite the fact that I kept busy, I got very little accomplished. By the end of the second month I began noticing how difficult even the smallest tasks became. Keeping my mind focused on any one thing became a challenge. I felt sometimes as if I was losing my mind. A task that took an hour suddenly became a three day long ordeal for me. I jumped from one thought to another; one task to another. I could barely focus on anything. But at the same time, I moved at a snail's pace. I have never experienced anything like this in my life. I hurt emotionally and physically.

It is during this phase that some bereaved individuals begin to make impulsive decisions. Mental health professionals warn not to make important life changing decisions for at least a year. Our fragile minds are in no state to make rational major decisions. We may find that we have regrets for those decisions later on down the road. The Compassionate Friends network discourages selling a home, changing jobs, divorcing, or engaging in compulsive spending until a year has passed. It is important to let the confusion of grief settle before we make major changes.

I walked on shaky ground trying to find answers. What I did not realize was how my brain would become so jumbled from the effects of grief. I was no longer in denial of her death but certainly in denial that I had received signs from her afterwards.

Depression sneaks up on you and takes you by surprise. I felt confused and had trouble concentrating. I constantly felt like my feet were embedded in concrete. I was always exhausted and my body ached. I barely slept and when I did, I did not dream. It was a restless sleep. I began to feel as if I was losing my mind.

In *Farewell, My Forever Child*, I described the strange world of confusion in the grieving process.

I realize in hindsight that I was very much in denial about Stephanie's dementia. The doctor had informed me of her worsening condition in 2011. But when Stephanie died in 2013, I remembered that conversation with the doctor taking place during the fall in 2012. I had completely confused the time frame as to how long ago she had been diagnosed. That is how denial works. We see through rose colored glasses until later on when we can assess in retrospect with a clearer understanding. When she died, a friend who was in the medical field reminded me of the prognosis pointing out that I might find solace in that she avoided a slow deterioration from the Alzheimer's. She was going into her second year of having dementia but my mind had distorted the time frame to make it more comfortable for me. This is common in grief. This is why the griever often feels as if he/she is going crazy. Details are scrambled; time frames skewed; and information is shrouded in the fog of grief.

As grief progresses into depression, the fog gets denser. It was all I could do get through a day much less actually be productive. I felt like I was stuck in a nightmare; one from which I could not awaken.

The third month was harder than ever. There was no more denial, no more guilt, and no anger. There was just hard core pain; an indescribable sadness that cut me to my core. Every night I sobbed until I fell asleep. The pain was raw; like a gaping wound. I rode the wave of despair, every day and night. I cried when I needed to release the pain. I accepted the fact that I would never get over this loss; I would never stop missing my daughter. I gave myself permission to be depressed regardless of the fact that others were uncomfortable with it.

My advice to those who are going through the loss of someone they love is to deal directly with it. If you feel angry, allow yourself to be angry. If you feel like crying, give yourself permission to cry. If you try to repress the grief it will only rear its ugly head later on. Grief is not something you get over, it is something you have to work through.

During this time it is important to take care of yourself. You will need more sleep. If you are fortunate enough to have a schedule that allows you to get extra rest, take advantage of that. Take vitamins and eat well. It is crucial to allow yourself to heal at your own pace. Do not force yourself to engage in activities that you don't feel ready to attempt. Take some down time. Take time to meditate. Quiet alone time will help process your feelings. Be easy with yourself. If you have a partner, understand that he/she is also hurting and has suffered a loss, as well as the children in the family. Share feelings with other family members and include them in grief groups and counseling sessions.

When Stephanie died, many people expressed that her sudden, unexpected death was a *blessing in disguise*. One friend, a nurse who worked with mentally disabled people, even called it *a gift from God*. At first it was extremely distressing to hear this. The words cut through me like a knife. But given the fact that her prognosis was not positive, I understood what she meant. My mind understood that my child was spared much suffering both mentally and physically by her sudden passing. But my heart still ached over the loss. I could never bring myself to feel that her untimely death could be a blessing. But at the same time, I would have not wanted to see her slowly destroyed by Alzheimer's disease either. I was to some degree relieved that she was spared unnecessary suffering though I still missed her desperately.

Dr. Raymond Moody has worked with the bereaved for over forty years. He is also responsible for coining the phrase, *near death experience*. He discovered that quite often, people have symptoms of the illnesses of their deceased loved ones usually occurring at anniversary of their death. This *anniversary reaction* as he calls it is completely subconscious. Some have even died on the anniversary of a significant loved one. In his documentary, *When Loved Ones Die*, Dr. Moody recalls how several relatives died on anniversary dates of one another. He noted that both Thomas Jefferson and John Adams died on the 50th anniversary of the signing of the Declaration of Independence. Could these situations be purely coincidental? Or is there some rhyme and reason to when we die and how close we die to someone else?

Even years after a child has passed away, a parent will begin to relive the initial stages of grief at the anniversary of the death. This can be extremely disturbing to a parent but is a completely normal reaction. Even if the mind does not consciously remember the approaching anniversary, the body does. It is for this reason that avoiding or denying grief can be detrimental to our health.

My daughter died several weeks before her thirtieth birthday. Instead of throwing a party, I decorated her grave. I felt as if I would die myself. Over the next couple of months, I faced my first Easter and my first Mother's Day without her. Her birthday was without a doubt the hardest to face.

Episodes of severe depression can occur or worsen during holidays. Birthdays, Christmas, and the anniversary of the death are often the most difficult. Any holiday or family celebration can become living hell to a grieving parent. After someone's death, our lives become divided into two separate time frames; the period in time when that person was alive, and the period after that person's death. Everything for me is now measured in before Stephanie died, and after Stephanie died.

Chapter Four
Hauntings

"They say that shadows of deceased ghosts do haunt the houses and the graves about, of such whose life's lamp went untimely out, delighting still in their forsaken hosts." ~ Joshua Sylvester

Even though I was doing everything I could to grieve in a healthy, productive way, I felt as if I could not shake the *grief crazies*. I did not know if half of what I was experiencing was real or imagined. I questioned every thought, every feeling I experienced. This was particularly unnerving when I began to experience what Dr. Kubler-Ross refers to as *visual hauntings*. Commonly during extreme episodes of grief, the bereaved will see the deceased loved one or reminders of that loved one all around.

I had spent the better part of the past twenty years researching paranormal phenomena, investigating haunted locations, writing books on hauntings, producing and appearing in various television shows, and speaking at conferences on the subject. By most definitions, I was an expert in the field. My work was recognized world-wide. Stephanie had accompanied me on numerous locations during filming sessions. She was more than just sensitive to spirits; she was a medium. I always felt as if she walked in this world and that one.

In my book, *Searching for Spirits: The Ultimate Guide for Ghost Hunters,* I recalled one of her experiences on the set for *Haunted New Orleans* television show:

Kalila Smith with Stephanie Link

During filming of this investigation, I had my daughter, Stephanie, with me. As we filmed in one room, I happened to notice out of the corner of my eye that she was standing in the hallway with her eyes wide and her hands over her mouth. She was pointing at something down the hallway. When I asked her about it she described a man wearing a dark suit with dark hair who appeared to be angry. Later that night, two of my paranormal investigators, Jonathan and Adam, found one of the photo albums of the original owners. One photo was that of a man who fit that description. When we showed the photograph to Stephanie, she exclaimed, "That's him! The angry man."

There are many types of hauntings. The majority of hauntings are residual; there is no intelligent entity present but rather an energetic impression left in an area. The causes can be anything from a trauma or strong emotion to a repetitive action such as a shutter slamming over and over again. Most residual hauntings are so subtle that in the normal course of daily activity, they often go unnoticed. Because residuals are so inconspicuous, it is easy for the conscious mind to rationalize away their existence.

The active, or intelligent, haunting is best described as a disembodied spirit of someone who was once human. We have several layers to our bodies. We have a physical body, but it does not stop there. We also have an astral body, an ethereal body and a spirit body. All of our bodies are comprised of energy. This energy extends from our bodies as far as seventeen feet, called an *aura*. Some people can even see auras. When the physical body dies, the energy within leaves its shell and continues to live in another state outside of what is physical reality. For the most part, active hauntings are seen in the peripheral vision. Many people assume that they are *seeing things* when in fact they have witnessed a ghost. One misconception is that intelligent entities are stuck on our physical plane. We know now that this is not necessarily so. There are several planes of existence and some of these spirits choose to remain closer to the physical plane of existence for their own personal reasons. In many of the near death experiences that have been documented throughout time, experiencers report going through a dark void of some kind and being aware of other spirits present. Some are moving toward the next level of existence, others are not moving, but most agree, it is by choice. If this is true, then what we once called a ghost is simply the spirit body of a person who had chosen to not move forward.

A crisis apparition is an apparition that appears shortly before or after death, or at the precise time of death. I have found that these recently departed spirits can appear to take care of any unfinished business and saying goodbye for several days after death.

These types of hauntings do not mean that the person's spirit is trapped on the earth plane or that they are going to remain earthbound for an extended period of time. These spirits remain earthbound long enough to visit loved ones, say their goodbyes, and give last minute messages to those who were emotionally close to them, then the move on. Many believe that all spirits stop in and say goodbye or give messages but that's not necessarily the case. This belief often leads to disappointment when a loved one passes. Of the ones who do, this manifestation can appear in various forms.

Nina De Santo is a member of the Eastern Pennsylvania Paranormal Society. One of the reasons she wound up investigating the paranormal was because of an experience she had a while before, when she was the owner of a hair salon in New Jersey. She was interviewed at the time by John Blake of CNN in September, 2011. Blake wrote:

Nina De Santo was about to close her New Jersey hair salon one winter's night when she saw him standing outside the shop's glass front door.

It was Michael. He was a soft-spoken customer who'd been going through a brutal patch in his life. His wife had divorced him after having an affair with his stepbrother, and he had lost custody of his boy and girl in the ensuing battle.

He was emotionally shattered, but De Santo had tried to help. She'd listened to his problems; given him pep talks, taken him out for drinks.

When De Santo opened the door that Saturday night, Michael was smiling.

"Nina, I can't stay long," he said, pausing in the doorway. "I just wanted to stop by and say thank you for everything."

They chatted a bit more before Michael left and De Santo went home. On Sunday she received a strange call from a salon employee. Michael's body had been found the previous morning -- at least nine hours before she talked to him at her shop. He had committed suicide.

If Michael was dead, who, or what, did she talk to that night?

"It was very bizarre," she said of the 2001 encounter. "I went through a period of disbelief. How can you tell someone that you saw this man, solid as ever, walk in and talk to you, but he's dead?"

Today, De Santo has a name for what happened that night: "crisis apparition." She stumbled onto the term while reading about paranormal activities after the incident. According to paranormal investigators, a crisis apparition is the spirit of a recently deceased person who visits someone they had a close emotional connection with, usually to say goodbye.

She said she checked with Michael's relatives and poured through a coroner's report to confirm the time of his death, which was put at Friday night -- almost 24 hours before she saw him at her salon on Saturday night.

She said Michael's body had been discovered by his cousin around 11 Saturday morning. Michael was slumped over his kitchen table, dead from a self-inflicted gunshot.

De Santo was baffled at first, but now she has a theory.

Michael started off as a customer, but she became his confidant. Once, after one of her pep talks, Michael told her, "You make me feel as if I can conquer the world."

Maybe Michael had to settle affairs in this world before he could move on to the next, De Santo said.

Afterlife Mysteries Revealed

"A lot of times when a person dies tragically, there's a certain amount of guilt or turmoil," she said. "I don't think they leave this Earth. They stay here. I think he kind of felt he had unfinished business. He needed to say goodbye."

And so he did, she said. This is how she described their last conversation:

As they chatted face to face in the doorway of her shop, De Santo said they never touched, never even shook hands. But she didn't remember anything unusual about him -- no disembodied voice, no translucent body, no "I see dead people" vibe as in the movie "The Sixth Sense."

"I'm in a really good place now," she recalled him saying.

There were, however, two odd details she noticed at the time but couldn't put together until later, she said.

When she first opened the door to greet Michael, she said she felt an unsettling chill. Then she noticed his face -- it was grayish and pale.

And when she held the door open for him, he refused to come in. He just chatted before finally saying, "Thanks again, Nina."

Michael then smiled at her, turned and walked away into the winter's night.

A common theme for the crisis apparition is to awaken to find a departed loved one sitting on the edge of the bed wanting to speak. Other themes include symbols manifesting that have particular meaning to the departed and the receiver, and there can also be dream manifestations. This is a common manifestation for after death communications, ADCs. Usually these types of visual communications occur very close to the death of the person or near an anniversary of the death.

By the end of month three I had gotten myself through the denial and shock stage. I knew and understood that she was never coming back. What I could not find was peace. During those first few weeks, I saw visual hauntings of her everywhere. I work in the French Quarter and rarely see individuals with Down syndrome, but suddenly everywhere I turned there were families with DS children. One day as I was getting out of my car, a boy with DS and his family stood directly across from me. Another day, a girl in a purple cap and gown followed her mother down the street as I passed. The following day, as I sat at a stop sign and family passed with a DS child. A band playing in a parade came past but there were no DS children. However one of the boys playing drums was wearing a sock monkey hat just like one Stephanie wore before her death. It seemed that around every turn was a painful reminder of my loss.

A friend once told me that after her father died, she saw what looked like him on a streetcar that was going by. She explained that her father had a very distinct profile and shape of his head. She describes not seeing someone who looked like but his physical presence on that streetcar. She is convinced without a doubt that is was his apparition that she saw shortly after his death.

A haunting can be a feeling or a presence of a loved one that is felt in familiar places such as the person's home or some place that they frequented. Such a presence could be the spirit of that individual or merely their energetic impression still lingering. Often, it is their actual presence, especially if it is soon after they departed. Some hauntings can be heard like a voice or laugh of that person. Usually these types of communications that are experienced early on serve to give comfort to the bereaved. They let us know that our loved one still exists or that they are okay. Sometimes they might have a specific message to take care of unfinished business. Other times they want forgiveness. The signs we receive early on are there to comfort us.

Sometimes visions occur soon after the death or at a significant time related to the death. Certain weird circumstances that follow a death of a loved one defy scientific explanation. My dear friend, Gary, died eight months after he appeared to me in a dream telling me good-bye. Stephanie followed him to the grave exactly eight months after his death, and on the eve of his birthday.

Systemic therapist, Hugh Palmer did not give a lot of credence to the afterlife until his father died and he began to see visions. He was gracious enough to share his experience and his report with me. He wrote in his article, *Between the material and the supernatural: Therapeutic implications of bereaved individuals experience of contact with the deceased person:*

Recent texts on bereavement (for example, Worden 2003), can be seen to treat grief as if it were an illness, with therapeutic models constructed to provide a path to recovery; identifying stages of grief before a resolution that culminates in the redirection of emotional energy elsewhere. More recently, the idea of 'continuing bonds' (Klass, Silverman & Nickman, 1996) and some social constructionist, narrative therapists (for example, Michael White, 1989; Hedtke &Winslade, 2004), offer ways for the bereaved individual to maintain a relationship with the dead person. Many bereaved people report sensing the presence of a deceased relative or friend and most commonly this occurs in dreams. Traditional grief literature describes these experiences as symptoms of grief or even 'hallucinations'. However, in popular literature they are attributed to 'after life communication' or sometimes 'after death communication' (for example, Newcomb 2007).The dichotomy between 'material' and 'supernatural' (Bennett & Bennett 2000) explanations for this type of experience may hamper useful conversations between therapists and clients. Discussing what might be considered as paranormal or hallucinatory experiences may be avoided (by both therapist and client) in therapy and clients may not bring these issues for fear of being judged as crazy. However, these experiences can have very healing effects, occasionally radically transforming views about life, death and spirituality, so that discussing them in a therapeutic climate may be helpful in the grieving process. Therapeutic conversations that are supportive of maintaining and developing a relationship with the deceased person need to incorporate discussion about client's experiences of sensing their presence.

Up until 1995, I had developed an epistemology that pretty much was in line with Bateson's idea of immanence. It seemed to me that mind was located in the relationship between body and environment, and there was nothing more than that. No spirit,

Kalila Smith with Stephanie Link

nothing transcendent. Then my father died. He'd had surgery three years previously for a melanoma which had required considerable plastic reconstruction and, whilst never as able to get around as much, for three years had been reasonably happy. Then he began to get back pain and, in a matter of weeks, was very ill, being cared for at home (luckily the local GP was experienced in palliative care) having developed metastases in his bones. I remember just before he died, he told me about his past, especially his childhood and how he and his younger sister were evacuees and shunted all over during the war. I'd heard these stories before and had a feeling that there was something else he wanted to tell me, but he was holding back. I didn't press him though. There was one thing I did know about his past, but it was unspoken between us; one particular event that had taken place around ten years previously which I had put down to an aberration on his part. I had seen him in a bar in our home town which was commonly known to be a gay venue. I knew from his response at the time that he was terribly embarrassed that I had seen him there. Later that evening, following out conversation, Dad slipped into unconsciousness and he died two days later.

Both I and my mother were with him as he died, and we both commented on the sensation of something filling the room and then moving off away and out of the house. Looking at his body, I felt that it was simply a shell; 'Dad' was no longer there. His body looked like a younger, more peaceful version of him. A few months later, I began to dream of him. He would appear in my dreams, where typically it would be a family occasion and he would be there, usually smiling, but never saying anything. In these dreams, rather surreally, we all knew he was dead, but accepted and enjoyed his presence. On several occasions, it was apparent that he wanted to communicate with me, but when he tried, his mouth was lined with what looked like black velvet, and no sounds could emerge. These dreams went on for some time, and I figured it was part of the grieving process, maybe something to do with 'unfinished business'. However, an opportunity presented itself when I was staying with my aunt and I asked her if there was a secret aspect to my father. Eventually, after a lot of thought, she admitted there was, that she knew about it, and wondered what had made me ask. I told her about the event I knew about, but not the dreams. She told me that my father was gay, and this had caused a lot of problems for him, as during the 1950's and 1960's homosexuality was viewed very negatively. The following weekend, I asked my mother about this and, while she needed to be certain what I was talking about before admitting anything, when she realized what I now understood about my father, the floodgates opened. I heard about the terrible difficulties they'd had, the struggles, and how they loved each other despite some considerable problems. She told me that, although Dad knew I was involved in teaching on HIV and AIDS and clearly not homophobic, nevertheless he couldn't risk my knowing and was scared that I would reject him.

I appreciated that my father was a lot more complex than I'd thought and also a lot stronger than I ever could imagine. I now had a sense that the things he'd been trying to tell me in my dreams had, at last, been said. At this point, I suppose it was convenient (and reasonable)for me to assume that the dreams were simply part of my grieving and based in part on the event that had happened many years ago. This assumption, however, was about to change along with my thinking about life after death when, a few weeks later, we went for a meal with some friends and were happily enjoying a post meal glass of wine when I became aware of a presence in the room. I remember thinking 'It feels like Dad is here' and saying so. The others laughed, but then I distinctly saw my father, sitting in an armchair, grinning from ear to ear! Whilst appearing transparent, he was wearing a familiar tweed jacket, and looked surprisingly well for a ghost. I told the others that I could actually see him, and pointed to the chair he was in. The others thought this was a hoot and that clearly I was off my trolley. My friend's wife went and sat on the chair, as if to say there was nothing there. I was laughing by now, because my father's grin was even wider, and he evidently found the situation funny. I could still see him superimposed over her, still grinning. Then he faded, and I became aware that he was in front of me, and slightly above my head height. Rather than being able to see him, I had a sensation of him being right in front of me, that he was aware of my life; the mistakes I had made, the good things I had done and, above all, an overwhelming sense of love. It was as if he could see right into my life and accepted and loved me for who I was. And I sensed that he knew that the love was reciprocated and he was glad that I now knew the story he had been unable to tell me when he was alive. I tried to explain what was going on to the others who by now were feeling a little unsettled and wondering if I was completely mad. My friend asked out aloud if my Dad would let them know he was there. I remember the look on their faces when, seconds later, there was an extremely loud rapping on their back door. They were mortified and scared. I was still laughing, still feeling bathed in the incredible sense of love and acceptance I had been shown. We opened the back door and peered outside. On their lawn, several of their children's toys and balls had been laid out in a perfectly straight line. I tried to reassure the others that everything was fine, but they were pretty shaken. They still talk about that night! Following that evening, my dreams subsided and I felt that my father was moving on. I recalled as a child I once asked him to let me know he was alright after he died. He had kept to his word. And I no longer believed that once we died that it was over. I became convinced that there is something about us that is transcendent, and I had direct experience of it. Since then, nearly 12 years later, I have heard many similar stories to my own; most notably recently when one of my friends told me about the dreams she had of her son who died unexpectedly in February 2007. In one dream, she saw him as if he was outside their house and, although he did not speak to her, he smiled and waved through the window, which she found very comforting. From anecdotal evidence, it would appear that there are certain patterns common to these dreams; often there is a metaphorical barrier between the dreamer and the departed person, for example windows between the two or the communication takes place over dreamed telephone conversation. Another pattern is the belief that the dream is

Afterlife Mysteries Revealed

somehow different to normal dreams, often accompanied by a powerful sense of love or connection with the departed person.

Almost one year to the date of Gary's anniversary of his death, I experienced visual hauntings of him. Ten days before the anniversary date, I saw a man come through the doors at the patio of a local French Quarter restaurant. He walked briskly though the double doors and out of the corner of my eye, he looked like him. Later, when I passed the same guy at the bar, I could clearly see that he looked nothing like my friend. But during that split second that he burst through the doors, he did. Then an hour later, as I waited on the steps of Jackson Square to begin a tour, I saw a different man, same height and build as my friend, walk directly through the square. He wore solid black jeans, cowboy boots, a black cowboy hat, and black shirt. He even walked like him. I had been talking to someone at the time and was thrown completely off by the sight of what looked exactly like my deceased friend walking by. I lost my train of thought and watched silently as this person disappeared into the crowd. This type of experience is not uncommon according to experts. These sightings at the time only served to throw me deeper into the depression of grief.

As I continued to fumble my way through my grief, the pain became even more raw and unbearable. I could never have my child back in this life, but knowing that she still existed, in a good place, and was with others who loved her, would help me cope with the loss. As I floated aimlessly in my sea of despair I questioned all of my beliefs. Was I going insane? Were the past twenty years of my life just some ridiculous figment of my imagination? The more I panicked over where Stephanie had gone, the further away she became. I wondered if all of us, throughout time, made these things up because the pain of those we loved just disappearing into non-existence was more than any human could stand. My mania went from those thoughts to thoughts of there is no afterlife. There is nothing out there; no God; no heaven; it is all a fantasy to make us feel better. I could no longer be angry with God but I no longer was sure if I believed in such a being. I felt as if I was truly going insane. I buried myself in books on near death experiences, after death communications, and deathbed visions.

This behavior would seem odd to most people given my background and knowledge in this area. I am certain most people who knew me or were familiar with my work would agree that I might be the last person to doubt life after death. But the truth is this is the effect of intensive grief. I had lost loved ones before throughout my life but nothing compared to losing my child. Unless someone has experienced this extreme type of grief it is impossible to comprehend. I doubted everything that I had ever believed. I also doubted everything that everyone was telling me at the time. I needed confirmation after confirmation for anything to sink in. I truly felt as if I was going insane.

A loss to this degree is life changing, especially if the loss is child. The parent who loses a child loses a lot more. An identity is lost. In my case, I had been my daughter's caretaker for almost thirty years; now that attachment to her had been severed. Not only was a significant person whom I loved very much gone, but the identity connected with that person had also died. Just as she had transformed into another level of existence, I was becoming a new person on this level. At that moment in time, I did not like what was happening. It was as if I was falling and did not know where I would land.

Chapter Five
NDEs: Are They a Sign of an Afterlife?

"He whose head is in heaven need not fear to put his feet into the grave." ~ Matthew Henry

I began my research of near death experiences (NDEs) several years ago as I delved deeper into the paranormal realm. We all question what lies beyond this life at some point or another. This subject seemed like a logical place to find proof of an afterlife. I sifted through countless case studies conducted over the past several decades. These were cases where people were pronounced clinically dead, had profound experiences, then returning to tell of it.

Dr. Raymond Moody wrote *Life after Life* in 1975. In it, he recounted many near death experiences from various people from all walks of life. Their experiences included some common traits. The first thing that many people described was an out of body experience. Nearly all of them recalled seeing their bodies on the hospital bed or surgery table, depending on where the experience took place, and they realized that they must have died. They did not feel any pain. In fact, most remembered feelings ranging from calmness to elation. Many reported heightened senses. They see, hear, smell, and feel things more vividly than before. They were aware of everything going on around them; yet, were not afraid.

Each of them described a buzzing sound inside their heads. Dr. Moody specifically noted that many people considered it to be uncomfortable or annoying. Others described the sound of tinkling bells or wind chimes in the distance. Several mentioned that they heard beautiful music. There is also a *rushing sound* shortly thereafter accompanied by feeling like they are being pulled into a dark tunnel. One man described the tunnel like an amusement park roller coaster ride.

Father Cedric Pisegna, a Catholic Priest, wrote *Death, The Final Surrender*. It is his personal memoir of his own NDE that resulted in his commitment to later becoming a priest. His message is very to the point; *your soul will never die*.

His experience in the tunnel is one of resistance as a young man. He wrote, "I vividly remember that I fought going through that tunnel. I am used to being in control and fear loss of it. That is exactly what I experienced then; the complete loss of control. I didn't know where I was, where I was going, or what was going to happen to me. In some ways it was like the take-off roll of an airplane. There was no turning back and no way out. I had to surrender to what was occurring to me. I hated the feeling of being out of control, but I didn't have the strength to resist because I was drawn down that passageway by a power much greater than myself" (49).

In *Embraced by the Light,* Betty Eadie described hearing a soft buzzing sound in her head then feeling *a surge of energy* that pulled her real self through her physical chest. As with many who have had NDEs, she became aware of having a *new body*. Again, this is a common theme. Some later talked of a type of body that they find difficult to describe but all felt much freer outside of the old physical body. Eadie was greeted by three spiritual beings dressed in robes that she believed were some sort of guardian spirits. She described them as *ministering angels* who communicated telepathically to her.

The tunnel is very dark and void. Many described it as spiraling and there is a feeling of moving through it. Despite that fact that its description sounds frightening, those who have experienced it report feelings of well-being and pleasure. Several sources indicated that most people were aware of others being in the tunnel and that some were not moving forward.

Betty Eadie wrote, "I felt as if I had been swallowed up by an enormous tornado. I could see nothing but the intense, almost tangible darkness. The darkness was more than a lack of light; it was a dense blackness unlike anything I had known before" (37).

She also described knowing that she could stay there if she chose to. She became aware of others in the tunnel; humans and animals. She was also aware that there were some in the tunnel that were not moving forward. She again mentioned that there was no fear.

She wrote, "I had never felt greater tranquility in my life" (Eadie, 39).

At the end of the tunnel is a bright light to which most feel drawn. Inside this light is where most described meeting a loving being and a feeling of *coming home*. Many called the being God or Jesus; others, simply a being of light and love. These individuals reported feeling unconditional love, compassion, and acceptance from this being of light. A majority of the cases reported some sort of life review taking place. As with the tunnel, it is remembered as a pleasant event, not judgmental at all. In certain cases, the individual was asked if they wanted to stay or return, but some cases reported being told it was not their time, and that they had to return to this life.

Betty Eadie wrote, "I saw a pinpoint of light in the distance. The black mass around me began to take on more of the shape of a tunnel, and I felt myself traveling through it at an even greater speed, rushing toward the light. I was instinctively attracted to it, although again, I felt that others might not. As I approached, I noticed the figure of a man standing in it, with the light radiating all around him" (40).

A great deal of people described seeing their loved ones inside the light, those who had passed before were there to greet and comfort them. The main component in all of the NDEs was that these people returned with a more purposeful life, a renewed faith in God, and a desire to share their experience with others.

I found some religious sources criticizing NDEs as hallucinations, caused by evil influences, or even the devil. However, if evil spirits were to blame, those who returned from their experiences would not be compelled to live their lives with a renewed faith in God. Most of those who experienced a near death encounter returned with not only renewed faith but a complete change in their life priorities. Most are far less materialistic upon their return realizing that love and our relationships with others are the most important things in life. Without fail, they all return without fear of death. And they all feel compelled to share their experiences with others.

Another common experience is some sort of life review. Most who have experienced a NDE report going over their life experiences as part of learning from them. The way Father Cedric explained it was that he became more aware of who he was as a person rather than showing each deed. As a twenty-year-old young man, he realized how selfish and narcissistic he had been for most of his life. He returned from his experience with not only renewed faith in a loving God but a completely different priority for his life's work. No longer did he desire to pursue a career in business and earthly possessions. He made a complete turn-around, becoming a priest.

There are some who feel there are scientific explanations for NDEs that disprove theories of an afterlife. In a three year study that began on heart attack patients in 2006, Dr. Sam Parnia of South Hampton University concluded, "evidence is now suggesting that mental and cognitive processes may continue for a period of time after a death has started." Dr. Parnia calls the experience as "essentially a global stroke of the brain. Therefore, like any stroke process, one would not expect the entity of mind/consciousness to be lost immediately." Some researchers believe that the experience could be caused from cerebral anoxia (lack of oxygen to the brain) and secretions from the pineal gland that occur at death, causing the brain to continue to function for a brief period of time, and certain symptoms such as a narrowing of vision and seeing a bright light are merely chemical reactions in the brain. Other researchers feel that they can prove that the experiences are very real.

In 1998, Dr. Jeffrey Long and his wife, Jody, began a research group called Near Death Experience Research

Foundation documenting thousands of cases of NDEs. In all of Dr. Long's published works, it is clear that he disagrees with this possible explanation. Dr. Long insists that these individuals have *vivid* memories of experiences that would be considered *medically inexplicable* due to lack of brain function. He further stated that numerous case studies involved people who were born blind and reported *seeing* things that would be impossible for them to have knowledge of without sight.

In Paul Perry's documentary, *The Afterlife*, Dr. Long stated that he felt certain that life continues after death. He found significant similarities in the experiences during his study. He says that most of the experiencers report a *greater* level of consciousness during the NDE.

Dr. Long studied thousands of NDEs spanning the globe and determined that most were similar regardless of culture, religion, or geographic location. The experience almost always transforms people lives. Over ninety percent of the experiencers in Dr. Long's study reported seeing deceased loved ones. Some of these even saw people they thought were familiar, and did not recognize, but later determined through family photos that they were family that had died much earlier. These were people they did not know necessarily during their life.

In a recent study conducted in Belgium, neuropsychologist Vanessa Charland-Verville noted that those who have experienced a NDE have more vivid memories of the experience than most people do of real life experiences. She stated in an article for Real Science, "It's really something that stays in the mind of people as a clear trace, and it's even clearer than a real memory."

One of the most compelling cases for the NDE to validate an afterlife is that of Dr. Eben Alexander, a neurosurgeon who became comatose while battling an uncommon form of bacterial meningitis, which almost never occurs in adults. The part of his brain responsible for consciousness was not functioning, and the prognosis was very bleak. After a week, he regained consciousness, eventually retelling of a life changing experience that he recalled while in a coma. Although he was not clinically dead, as he was on life support systems, his brain was not functioning.

But despite this complete breakdown, Dr. Alexander returned to consciousness a week later to tell of his NDE. As with most people who have gone through such an experience, Dr. Alexander returned with a changed outlook on death and spirituality. His experience convinced him that life continued to exist in a different realm, and it continued to do so without brain activity.

In an attempt to learn more about NDEs, I decided to attend an Afterlife Conference, where both Dr. Moody and Dr. Alexander were speaking. I hoped to learn more about NDEs. I also hoped it would give me some solace about my daughter's death. I planned a trip with my sister-in-law who was still grieving my brother's death. We both hoped to return with answers that might make us find our losses a little more bearable.

I had also become aware that one of the experts in NDEs and ADCs actually lived very close to where I lived. Dr. Jeffrey Long practiced in Houma, LA. I contacted him in hopes of interviewing him in person about his thoughts on this subject.

Chapter Six
ADCs: Real Experiences or Figments of Our Imaginations?

"Has this world been so kind to you that you should leave with regret? There are better things ahead than any we leave behind." ~ C.S. Lewis

After death communications or ADCs have been documented countless times for many years. According to Bill and Judy Guggenheim, authors of *Hello from Heaven*, there are twelve main kinds of ADCs that are commonly experienced after the death of a loved one. The Guggenheim's recorded over three thousand cases of ADCs from people from all walks of life. The following list was based upon their research:

The most common type of ADC is sensing a presence: The bereaved individual feels the loved one nearby although that person is not seen or heard. Often times, the person experiencing this type of communication discounts the experience by thinking it is merely being imagined. Some sources related this more to memory than actual experience, but Dr. Kubler-Ross considered these experiences to defy explanation. They can be felt directly after a death and can continue on for years to follow. In *On Grief and Grieving*, Dr, Kubler-Ross and David Kessler refer to these types of ADCs as *hauntings*. For many people the word *haunting* might represent something frightening or disturbing so most people prefer to not think of their loved one as a haunting. Regardless of what you call it, it would represent a *kinesthetic* ADC, one that you feel.

Another common type of communication is actually hearing a voice of a loved one. Sometimes their voices are heard externally but often it's telepathically; we hear it in our minds. This can be extremely confusing and a cause of turmoil for a newly bereaved individual. Along with grief comes confusion, and often times the bereaved feels as he/she is going crazy. The bereaved individual often does not believe what he/she heard or felt. The important thing to remember is to trust your intuition and trust your senses.

The third type of ADC is called a *twilight experience*. This type of ADC occurs when in an altered state, such as just waking up, just falling asleep, during meditation, or praying.

A fourth type of ADC that is auditory is one that takes place over the phone. People have actually experienced a phone ringing only to pick it up and hear the voice of their loved on the other line. This often occurs very early on and is usually to relay a short message.

On the Guggenheim's website, www.after-death.com, an article from the Miami Sun-Sentinel by Donna Pazdera, March 3, 1998, recounting an eerie tale of telephone communication was posted:

The woman who called Jerrod Zelanka's house early Sunday was crying and her voice was faint. "I'm at the bottom of a dark hole," the woman said. Then the line went to static. Zelanka hit *69, a code used to automatically trace the call, but the number could not be pinpointed.

Now, Zelanka and others think that call somehow was made by his friend, Leah Jean Ash, 20, after she and a friend had an accident on an all-terrain vehicle late Saturday. Ash, of Boca Raton, was a passenger on the three-wheel vehicle driven by Kenneth Coppolo, 33, of Deerfield Beach. Both were found dead early Sunday on the bank of a drainage canal after an accident.

The strange part is, neither Ash nor Coppolo carried a cellular phone that night, Parkland Police Chief Steve List said. Divers from the Broward Sheriff's Office checked the shallow canal on Monday to see whether there was a telephone, but found nothing, List said. Police are getting a subpoena to obtain the telephone records of calls, made that night to Zelanka's house, List said.

The accident happened toward the end of a rainy evening during which 6 friends took turns riding the Yamaha Banshee 350cc at a construction site for Heron Bay north of Holberg Road between Pine Island and Nob Hill roads in Parkland. Coppolo, whom friends said was an experienced all-terrain vehicle driver, apparently was blinded by the rain and made a turn while traveling about 30 mph. When the two didn't return, Mike Taylor, Ash's boyfriend, began to worry. He and the others called police and tried looking for them in the dark. Finally, about 6 a.m. on Sunday, Zelanka, 20, of Boca Raton and a schoolmate of Ash's, found the bodies after a two-hour search in his four-wheel-drive truck.

Some people feel the touch of their lost loved one. People have reported feeling a tap, a caress, or a hug from those who have crossed over. Several weeks after my daughter had died, I was lying in bed crying as I often did, and suddenly I felt a very slight touch on my hair and thought I heard a faint whisper say, *Mommy.*

She had a very light touch in life so of course it was extremely subtle. She would not come across very blatant since she was not a very aggressive person during her life. Everything about her was very gentle and child-like.

A very common type of ADC involves smelling a fragrance associated with a deceased loved one. That smell could be their perfume or after-shave lotion, cigar or cigarette smoke, powders, or favorite flowers. The olfactory ADC is one of the most common types of experiences to receive from the other side. Many residual hauntings are experienced through the sense of smell. I have often told people "you will smell something long before you hear it or see it."

There are a variety of visual experiences that can have been reported throughout time. These can be either actual visions as discussed earlier or as a picture in one's mind.

Kalila Smith with Stephanie Link

Some people see a transparent mist or even full body apparitions of the loved one. Some visitations of full body apparitions have also communicated verbally. One thing that the Guggenheim's noted was that even in the case of after death appearances the loved one "always appears in good health and whole regardless of their cause of death."

Many ADCs appear in dreams. Unlike normal dreams, ones that are truly communications with the other side are not full of symbols and hard to make sense of. They are usually extremely intense and very real. They are also remembered in great detail unlike a normal dream.

Several months after my friend Gary had passed away, I had a dream where I was taken to a large domelike, white building by some sort of spirit being. She was tall and did not speak. She wore all white and had long flowing dark hair. She pointed into the round fishbowl-like windows and I looked inside. I saw Gary dressed in white linen. His bare feet stood upon wood floors. His musical instruments were there in the room and he was surrounded by birds; beautiful yellow and white birds. He was laughing and feeding the birds. He looked very happy and content. I went to tap on the glass and the spirit stopped me. Without actually speaking, she let me know that it was not allowed. I had to be happy just seeing that he was happy. Then I woke up.

Later I told his sisters of the dream. They both agreed that the symbols in the dreams had meaning. He had made comments during his life about *living in a fishbowl* which explained the windows. The white linen, they explained, was a shirt that he loved to wear. One sister told me that he was wearing it one day and did not want to wear a seatbelt because it would wrinkle the shirt. Then at a red light he decided it was better to have wrinkles then blood and he put the belt on. Within a few moments he was hit by another driver and was glad he had buckled up. They confirmed that my dream about him was a valid communication.

Other types of ADC are the ones that involve physical phenomena. Electrical devices turn on and off, lights blink, and sometimes physical objects will be moved. There are also those associated with symbols. Of the many symbols associated with ADCs, some of the more common ones are butterflies, rainbows, and many species of birds, animals, flowers, and inanimate objects, coins, pictures or even license plates. According to Dr. Jeffrey Long who has collected over two thousand ADCs on his web site for the *After Death Communication Research Foundation,* www.adcrf.org, the most common symbols for ADCs are rainbows and butterflies.

The Guggenheims recommend having a pen and paper near the bed in the event of dream ADCs. All sources that provide information on ADCs reported that they are usually positive and help reduce grief and give comfort to those who are bereaved. Unfortunately, many people like me, in the very beginning are so deep in grief that unexpected or sudden ADCs at first can seem frightening or disturbing. One thing I did find out after several months was that intense grief, depression, or hysteria will prevent noticing ADCs. Many of the ADCs that I experienced early on were realized long after they happened because at the time, I was not ready to accept them. By accepting the ADC as coming from a deceased loved one, we have to have already accepted their death. This can be a difficult time early on when we are still in the grips of denial and shock.

Many famous people have talked of their own ADCs with deceased loved ones. The Guggenheim's documented several of these on their web site.

Michael Jordan believes his father communicates with him when he needs advice. He stated, "When I feel confused about a decision and over a night's period, I feel like I've come up with a solution. I feel like I've gotten spiritual input from my father. It gives me the confidence to make a decision instinctively, whatever the decision may be, from signing a new contract to making a family decision."

In a 1996 Associated Press Article, singer Barbara Streisand reported that she believed that her father inspired her from the grave for her movie, Yentl:

Streisand, whose father died when she was 15 months old, says in the November issue of George that she received two messages from her father at a seance in 1979, four years before "Yentl" was released.

"The first one was 'Sorry,' which was astounding because I was angry at him for leaving me," she said. "The second message was 'Sing proud.' I know it sounds crazy, but it was my father telling me to have the courage of my convictions. I made 'Yentl.' And I did sing proud."

At the time, Streisand said she was trying to decide whether to direct and star in "Yentl," a story of a Jewish girl who disguises herself as her dead brother Anshel so she can study to become a rabbi.

A few days before the séance, she made her first visit to her father's grave, which was next to that of a man named Anchel.

"To me this was a sign that I should make this movie," said Streisand, who appears on the cover of the political magazine dressed as Betsy Ross.

Former Beatle Paul McCartney is convinced that the spirit of his former wife, Linda, lives on. He told reporters that he sometimes sees a white squirrel in the forest and he believes that it is Linda's spirit.

During the first few weeks that I experienced ADCs from Stephanie, I was so confused from grief that I not only questioned their reality, but often completely dismissed them. This is what grief does. It is very common to become completely confused in the early stages of grief and have difficultly deciphering what is real and what is imagined. The griever questions everything. Life itself becomes surreal, and the griever floats in a dreamlike existence between the waves of pain. It becomes necessary to validate experiences again and again. Only in hindsight was I able to appreciate the signs my daughter gave to me in the very early days of my loss.

Signs from our loved ones give us hope and help us heal. They are a crucial part of finding acceptance at the end of our grieving process.

Chapter Seven
My Early Signs

"My view of the afterlife is that it's made of different levels, depending on how spiritual a life we live."~
John Edward

Dr. Moody reported that of the many signs that people see after a loved one dies, unusual behavior of an animal, often a bird, is one of the most common ones. In his DVD, *When Loved Ones Die*, he stated that a bereaved family member usually "intuitively knows that the bird has something to do with the deceased loved one." I didn't experience any activity from a bird when my daughter passed away, but I did experience very unusual behavior from a neighborhood cat. I own several rescue animals, four of which are cats. One in particular was specifically her cat. She was a feral kitten that my ex-husband rescued and gave to Stephanie. The cat became very connected to her. They were inseparable. Oddly enough, it was not her cat that displayed strange behavior (other than looking for Stephanie all over the house, obviously grieving her loss) but a neighbor's cat that never really had anything to do with either of us.

This cat visited my home three days after Stephanie died. I had just spent two days away from my home and returned after a friend came to stay with me. I was sitting at my computer by a window that faced my backyard. Typically, cats do not go into my backyard, not even my own cats due to the two large dogs that reside there. But this evening was different. The big dogs were inside when suddenly on the window sill, a small orange tabby with white markings and a blue collar around its neck, appeared. I recognized the cat as belonging to a neighbor who lives a few doors down from me. Earlier that day, I had been outside of the front of my house, and the cat appeared at my feet rubbing up against my legs, crying for attention. I thought it was odd since I had seen the cat down the street for many years and it had never been friendly to me. I leaned down and patted it before going back inside. If that wasn't strange enough, now it was at my window.

The cat was not just sitting on the window sill but frantically trying to get in through the window. It cried and clawed at my window screen relentlessly. I sat at my computer crying for my daughter, ignoring it at first. I was an emotional mess. All I could think of was, "The neighbor must have gone out of town and left her cat outside and it was hungry."

I hoped that she had not moved away, leaving the cat for someone else to care for. All I could imagine was the last thing I needed was another cat in my life. I got up and went outside and gave it some cat food and a pat on the head. Then proceeded to go inside and resume my crying. The cat ate the food then cried and clawed at my back door. Eventually, the cat went away. The next day I saw the cat back at my neighbor's house. When I tried to approach it, it ran from me as if it had no idea who I was. I have seen the cat since, but only sitting in my neighbor's yard. I later read somewhere that deceased loved ones sometimes early on appear in the form of an animal, and display unusual behavior. I felt awful at that point, of course. I worried that perhaps my daughter had tried to reach out to me and I ignored her. Then, of course, felt guilty because of it. Needless to say in my state of mind, this created much distress for me as I worried she didn't understand. Now of course I realize that if indeed she did use the cat as a vehicle to communicate, assuming that does happen, she should have known that I wasn't going to entertain bonding with a fifth cat that might possibly be searching for a new home. To this day, I cannot explain what happened that day with the cat.

I don't recall any type of animal encounters when either of my parents died, but I did have some animal encounters shortly after the death of my brother in 2008. As a young child, my brother would take me out in the yard at night to hunt for frogs, commonly found there. We had mimosa trees growing in our yard, and at night, they would be covered with frogs. My brother took me out every night and we would catch them. I'd play with them for a while then let them go, only to repeat it the following night. For my entire life, my brother would remind me of my frog-hunting days.

When I returned to work after my brother's funeral I was on St. Peter Street to do the usual tour set up. At some point, I realized that I had to go back to my car for a schedule. I went to the car, opened the passenger door, got what I needed and shut the door. As I walked away, I felt the need to look back. When I turned, I saw that my lights had turned on. They had not been on the moment before or I would have noticed it when I walked up the first time. The switch turns on manually. Shutting the passenger door could not have caused the switch to turn on. I immediately thought that my brother gave me the sign I had asked for, but was still a bit skeptical. So I told him, "Not good enough. You'll have to do better than that to convince me."

Later that evening, while conducting a tour, as I walked down Ursulines Street, I looked down and saw a large green tree frog hop across my foot and disappear into a drain. The Quarter is nothing but concrete, there is not even the slightest hint of grass growing or trees in the area; not a friendly environment for these creatures.

There are no green tree frogs in the Quarter. In fact, I had lived in Uptown New Orleans for twelve years and had never seen one. Not until I moved into St. John Parish did I see one from time to time. Prior to that, I had not seen any since my childhood. I believed that seeing one of those frogs crossing the pavement in the Quarter indicated that he had given me the sign I had asked for. Considerably larger than any I had ever seen, it convinced me that he made contact with me and found peace.

Later that evening, when I got home, at least a dozen green frogs covered my front door and a large dragonfly flew around them. Leave it to him to have to prove his point over and over again. That entire week, frogs greeted me on my door. After about a week of frog visitation, they went away. I remain convinced that these occurrences represented my big brother giving me the signs.

On the same night that the cat tried to get into my window, I had another strange frog encounter; at least I think it was a frog. My house guests had gone to bed and I was sitting at the computer because I was restless. All of the animals were asleep and the house was reasonably quiet. I got up and began to turn off lights in preparation for going to bed. All of a sudden, I heard the loudest sound coming directly from my front door. It sounded like a mammoth tree frog. I know that both of my guests were not asleep at this point, and their rooms faced the front of the house. One was next to the foyer. No one else heard this disturbing sound that lasted a minute or two. I stood frozen in the foyer.

Having grown up and lived for many years in a swamp, I was well aware of what a tree frog sounded like. This thing was definitely a frog sound but loud. I rarely feel fearful about things but at that moment, I felt terrified. Then the sound faded and I never heard it again. I wish I had opened the front door but I was so emotionally distraught, I just couldn't bring myself to investigate what the sound might be. It was extremely disturbing.

I also had an encounter with a bird after my brother passed away. In fact, after his death many people reported seeing hummingbirds which were his favorite birds. My brother's favorite book was *Jonathan Livingston Seagull.* He died of lung cancer. One day not too long after his death, I was visiting the beach. At the time I smoked. I lit up a cigarette while on the beach, and just as I went to take a drag of it, a seagull flew over me and dropped feces on my cigarette! I was convinced it was my brother telling me to stop smoking.

Not too long after my brother's death, I was driving out of my street and as I turned the corner, there on the golf course, in the middle of the morning, stood a full-grown bald eagle. I have lived here my entire life. I have never seen a bald eagle just standing around on a golf course. It just stood there, watching me. I stopped and watched it for a while, and then it flew away. My brother not only loved eagles but also worked his entire life as a federal agent for Homeland Security and Immigration. What bird could better represent him?

Shortly before the anniversary of Gary's death, I had just seen someone twice that evening that looked and walked exactly like him. As I stood on the steps of the square beginning a tour, a woman in the group pointed behind me and said, "Look at that bird, it's weird."

I turned around to see a great blue heron standing in the middle of Jackson Square. I live near the swamp and never see them there. They are usually deep in the swamp or down in the marshes along the coast; never in the city. It was just standing there looking at me.

In Native American paths, birds are believed to be messengers of the Great Spirit and the Ancestors on the other side. The blue heron is often associated with messages from the other side. It appeared again on the exact anniversary date, only it stood at the corner of my street on the golf course, right where the eagle stood after my brother's death. Five days later on the evening of his memorial tribute, I saw a great blue heron fly above my house as I left my driveway.

Dragonflies are also often associated with signs from loved ones. Interestingly, on the evening of my granddaughter's graduation, I was feeling especially sad that Stephanie was missing from a family celebration. When I arrived home that night, a large, black dragonfly had attached itself to my front door. I came in and out of the door several times, trying to disrupt it, but it wouldn't budge. It stayed there for hours. Many people interpreted this as a sign from Stephanie.

One odd thing that happened involving an animal after my daughter's death was the death of one of my dogs. Stephanie loved animals and since we had quite a few, she of course, had her favorites. Hunter was *her* cat and Jasmine was *her* dog. Jasmine was one of two golden retrievers that we had raised since they were puppies. One had been my other daughter's dog, but Jasmine came to Stephanie when she was only a five-week-old puppy. When Stephanie died, Jasmine and Layla were almost nine-years-old. Jasmine had some health problems that her sister dog did not share. She was already displaying signs of hip dysplasia and arthritis. She also had some metabolic issues. Even though both dogs were the same age and ate the same amount, Jasmine was significantly larger than the other; over one hundred pounds. Despite the health concerns, Jasmine seemed reasonably healthy otherwise.

Two months after Stephanie died, I found Jasmine dead on her bedding from no apparent cause. She had been happy and active the previous night when I came home from work, and in the morning, she was dead. She left as unexpectedly as Stephanie had.

I happened to be preparing to attend a convention in Memphis that weekend, and had the opportunity to speak with Missa Dixon; a pet psychic and author of *Interviews from the Ark,* a book written along with Joy Ward on animal communication. Missa had an interesting perspective on the situation. She explained to me that animals have specific purposes in this life and once that purpose has been fulfilled, the animal no longer remains in our physical world. Her theory was that possibly Jasmine's mission in this life was to be with Stephanie during her life. Once that mission was complete, Jasmine's job here on earth was done. It has been proven that animals do mourn for their lost owners, just as we mourn our losses. Missa believed that Jasmine decided to simply leave and join Stephanie on the other side.

In her book, Missa introduced a striped cat named Milo who talks of his *Young Mama* who possesses what he calls the *Paw of God.* Milo communicated through Missa. That meant that she was very special and God protected her. He described a pink light around her (Dixon/Ward, 67).

Butterflies are also often associated with messages from deceased loved ones. Interestingly, butterflies were a very common theme with my daughter. It seemed she was always drawing or coloring or making one in some sort of art project. Various people have reported seeing butterflies after the death of a loved one. I did have one incident that involved a butterfly. Shortly after her birthday which was March 1, I cut the grass in the backyard for the first time since the summer before. It was still unseasonably cool outside and was not officially spring quite yet. When I hit a patch of high grass, a large Monarch butterfly appeared and flew around my head. I found it odd as I had not seen any other butterflies that early in the season. A month later, I still had not. The butterfly theory seemed a bit obscure even for someone like me. But I have to admit that this bug's behavior was not typical of a butterfly.

A few weeks later, the Compassionate Friends chapter had their annual butterfly release to honor the children. When we opened our butterflies, they flew out, except one. The one my ex-husband opened flew out of its envelope, but landed on his thumb; and didn't want to leave. We took several photographs of the butterfly that sat quietly on his thumb for quite a few minutes. Eventually, it flew away, but again it displayed very odd behavior for a butterfly.

It was interesting to learn that part of the near death experience described by Dr. Eben Alexander in his *Proof of Heaven, A Neurosurgeon's Journey Into the Afterlife,* involved butterflies. Dr. Alexander described seeing butterflies. He also went into elaborate description of the clouds he saw while he was on the other side. He expressed being in awe of these clouds.

Oddly enough, when my therapist encouraged me to write a letter *from Stephanie* using my left hand; I wrote over and over the word *clouds*. At the time it didn't make sense until I started working on the artwork for the cover of this book. I took Stephanie's photo and superimposed it upon a flat background. I sat staring at it wondering what was missing. Then suddenly, the word *clouds* came into my mind. It was what we in Gestalt call the *aha* moment. It then made sense to me. The cover of the book needed to be clouds. I found a generic cloud background which ultimately became the book cover. When I learned of Dr. Alexander's story and his emphasis on the clouds he witnessed it solidified that perhaps my writing actually did include a message from my daughter not only instructing me on what the cover of this book should look like, but also expressing the same awe for clouds that she too saw.

Other common signs that many people consider communication from loved ones on the other side include: finding pennies or dimes in obscure places, feathers, images of hearts in clouds, finding rocks in the shapes of hearts, and sequences of numbers or names in odd places, and songs. Some people reported seeing a license plate that maybe had the person's name or nickname on it suddenly appearing on a vehicle directly in front of their car. When the Compassionate Friends displayed a photograph on their Facebook page to promote their annual walk, they posted a photograph of two walkers who had signs on their back with a child's name. Both walkers' signs said, *Steph*. I may not totally subscribe to these types of signs as concrete proof of after death communication (ADC), but it is awfully coincidental.

Many people have manifestations of televisions turning on, lights flashing, or other physical manifestations shortly after a loved one dies. Dr. Moody noted that most of the time, these occurrences follow the death of a child or very young person, and it is usually a sudden death. I didn't notice any specific experiences of this type but my older daughter, Chastity and my granddaughters had several profound experiences at their home. Stephanie adored her older sister and her nieces so it stood to reason that she would desire to spend some time with them before she moved on.

Chastity is not a person to give in to superstition or anything that might be construed as paranormal. She was a spiritual person, but her beliefs were very skeptical and rather conservative when it came to the spirit world. She is not the type of person to have paranormal experiences. But when her sister died, it seemed that her skepticism was challenged. She called me one day a few days after the funeral and told me that some strange things were happening at her house.

Chastity lives with my three grandchildren (her children) who are teenagers. They too were witnessing the same thing. She reported the swinging door that led to her kitchen opening and closing on its own several times. My youngest granddaughter, Brittany, had also experienced a couple of unexplained situations.

The first was when she attempted to dry a load of clothes and the dryer door opened by itself. This dryer had a door that snapped shut. It was physically impossible for it to open without being pulled from the outside. On another occasion, Brittany had opened a can of soda and took a sip then placed it on her dresser. She then left the room to go to the bathroom. When she returned, the can was still sitting on her dresser, only it was empty. She was alone in the house. This was the second time something happened involving soda pop. Several weeks before, I had left an open can of root beer on a table at my ex-husband's house in front of some flowers for Stephanie. He reported that the can was empty the next day and upside down on the table. Again, there was no one else in the home when this happened.

Chastity told me, "I can ignore that and even come up with logical explanations for it. Something happened that was very weird and I cannot explain it. Amber (her oldest child) was in the bathroom brushing her teeth and the toilet flushed on its own. Don't you think that's weird?"

"Maybe it's your sister," I answered, not knowing what else to offer.

"No, seriously, Mom, what do you think?" She asked again.

"I don't know," I said, "I'd like to think it's your sister but I'm very disappointed that she's not doing that here with me. I wonder if she's mad at me or something."

"Mom, really," she insisted "I mean, what do you think it is? Do you think something weird followed me home from the cemetery?"

My oldest daughter has one fear when it comes to the paranormal, and that's demons. She subscribes to the traditional Catholic school of thought that anything paranormal is demonic activity.

"If something followed you home, it's probably your sister telling you that she still is around," I assured her, still pondering in my mind why she wasn't flushing my toilets.

"What do *you* think it is?" I asked her.

"Well, I don't know, but what really has me thinking that it is something supernatural is that I know my computer's battery has run down. The computer just came on and I'm looking at the power cord across the room," she said.

"If I have to guess, I'm going to say it's your sister," I told her.

Several days later Chastity called me to ask if I had come over, entered her house then left. I had not, of course. She said that she and her boyfriend both heard the iron-gate unlock and open, then the front door open and shut. They both heard a female voice talking in the living room but were unable to distinguish what was said. In fact, she said that she had heard two distinctly different female voices. Thinking it was her oldest teenage daughter coming home, she went into the living room to greet her.

She saw her middle daughter, Megan, sitting quietly on the sofa watching a movie. She asked her if someone had come through the door and the response was shocking.

Megan responded, "Well, the door opened and closed but no one was there."

After that the activity stopped. It would seem that this activity would indicate that there is a period of transition when the deceased loved one is still present on the physical plane. But some ADCs are even more profound, such as those that appear as apparitions, and in dreams.

Chapter Eight
Dreams

"For death is no more than a turning of us over from time to eternity." ~ William Penn

Spirit communication often occurs during dreams. I have learned to distinguish when my dreams are ordinary dreams and when there are messages from spirit. The more in tune one is to receiving messages from spirit, the better one can interpret the nature of these dreams.

I was convinced without doubt that I had received a communication with Gary after his death. But later, I doubted everything because of losing my daughter. If ADCs were only fantasies, then it would seem that the opposite would be happening. I would be seeing her everywhere and in everything instead of not seeing her. If I was making this up I would create dreams of her; hallucinating signs all over the place. But I was getting nothing.

I began to think about all of the spiritual episodes that Stephanie had during *her* life. Sure, she could have been hallucinating as well, but certain things that she described were accurately in line with haunted locations. She had no knowledge of these stories to accurately describe people who allegedly haunted these locations. Little by little, I sifted through memories of situations where there was no physical explanation for what I had experienced.

When Stephanie died, I didn't get anything as clear from her like I did with Gary. This disturbed me deeply. She was the person who had been the closest to me. She lived with me longer than anyone. She accompanied me on various ghost hunts and knew that I would be expecting to hear from her. Naturally, I assumed that I would have more than the normal amount of communication from her. And I did; I just wanted more. The truth is that because she was my child and I was so shattered over her sudden death, nothing was good enough. I wanted her back. I wanted the life I had with her, alive and in my care. Nothing short of having my child here with me was going to satisfy me. I wanted my child, period. I began to doubt every single experience I had ever had, including those from Gary. I continued to be confused not sure of what was real. I experienced the insanity of grief.

The first real vision I had of her, was more of a twilight vision. I had awakened, but was very groggy. This happened directly after an auditory ADC. The night she died, I stayed overnight at my ex-husband's home. I was an emotional mess. She had literally been fine then dead within minutes. The loss was abrupt and shocking. I was inconsolable. My ex-husband had insisted that I stay at his home rather than in my house alone. I eventually was able to fall asleep in his guest bedroom. I was still exhausted from the week leading into her surgery when I barely got any sleep, so I slept rather soundly. I awakened to hearing her voice in my room. She sounded as if she was in another room, somewhat muffled. But it was clear that she called out to me. I heard her say, "Mommy, I found Baby Dog."

Baby Dog was her pet when she was a child. She never got over her death. She cried every time she saw a photo of Baby or saw a dog that looked like her.

I was definitely not asleep when I heard this. I was somewhat in an in-between state; the twilight state. I was just waking up and had not yet opened my eyes. But I felt certain that it was not a dream.

I then sat up in the bed and saw out of the corner of my eye a young woman sitting on the edge of the bed next to me. She wore a black and grey striped turtle-neck shirt, just like one that Stephanie owned, and a pair of jeans. She was very petite; maybe just about five feet tall, just as Stephanie was. Only this girl was much thinner than Stephanie had been. Because

Stephanie had Down syndrome, she had the typical weight issues from which many of them suffer. She had straight dark brown hair parted in the middle, and very fair skin, just like Stephanie. She had crystal blue eyes, and *her* nose. The rest of her face looked more like my other daughter or me when I was younger.

My first thought was, "It is Stephanie without Down syndrome."

She looked me directly in the face and put both hands up in the air, shrugged her shoulders, and a big smile crossed her face as if she was showing herself off and saying, "TA-DAAA, Look at me!"

Unfortunately, I was so distraught and still in shock that I almost fell off the bed, and burst into uncontrollable crying. Instead of being relieved to see what should have been a comforting vision of my child, it threw me into hysteria.

If indeed this was a visit from Stephanie, she looked more radiant and happier than I had ever seen her. For the next two days, I felt her energy all around my ex-husband's house. It was, after all, the house where she grew up. It felt as she was just in the next room. Being so soon after her death, it could have very well had just been my memory of her. But the image of her on the bed was real. I would imagine if I had made that up from memory, I would have seen her as I knew her, with Down syndrome. But I didn't. She looked like Stephanie but without the DS. Having never seen her like that it would have been impossible for that vision to have been a memory; either I really experienced seeing her apparition or my mind made it up. In the confusion of grief, I was not really sure which was true.

A few nights later, I saw her again. This time it was in a dream. For the last few months of her life, Stephanie spent many nights sitting at the kitchen table coloring. I would often awaken at around 4:00 AM and find her in there coloring alone at the table with her cat sitting next to her. In this particular dream, I walked down the hallway, but instead of finding my daughter coloring, she was seated there wearing the same outfit I had seen her in before, and she was painting her fingernails. It was very vivid. Unlike a normal dream, which is distorted and full of symbols, this was extremely real. Every detail of her clothing stood out. Her hair was shiny and bouncy; even her pink pearlescent nail polish shone vividly in my mind. She did not speak or even look up. She was just there, painting her nails with her cat sitting next to her. Seeing her like this prompted me to go buy her some pink nail polish and eye shadow and insist that the funeral home put it on her for her wake.

A couple of nights before her funeral, she appeared again in a dream. This time she spoke to me. But instead of a comforting message assuring me that she was fine, she was instructing me about her funeral. Again, she appeared as she looked on the edge of the bed. No longer a disabled little person with Down syndrome, she was a mature young woman. She told me, "Mom, you need to contact Roxanne and Crystal and tell them that I died. They need to know the arrangements."

"Okay, I have their numbers somewhere on the computer," I told her.

"Oh, and Ms. Vickie, Troy's mom, you need to call her, too," she instructed.

"I don't have her number," I said.

Then she handed me a small scrap of paper. It was jagged around the edges as if torn and tiny. On it a phone number was written in pencil. The weird part was that even though she appeared and spoke normally, the writing was like Stephanie's when she was alive. I recognized her handwriting. When I took the piece of paper from her hand, I woke up. I jumped out of bed and went to the computer and wrote down the number I had seen on that scrap of paper.

I proceeded to look up everyone else that she had named in the dream, and contacted each person, as she had instructed. Then I called the number I remembered from the dream. My heart pounded as I wondered if I had really gotten a visit from my baby. I stepped outside and slowly dialed the number then pressed the call button. The phone rang several times and a woman answered. I almost passed out when I asked for Vickie and she responded, "This is she."

Afterlife Mysteries Revealed

When I told my ex-husband about the dream, his explanation was that I had that number memorized in my subconscious. I'm sure that is entirely possible, but given the fact that I cannot recall any of my former telephone numbers from the 1990s, it seems unlikely that I would remember some else's.

Because the seed of doubt was planted, I began to wonder if my dreams were just made up. I called out to Gary and told him if he could hear me, that I wanted to know if my daughter was alright. I wanted confirmation through third parties, not dreams. Within forty-eight hours, I received an answer.

I received a text message from one of Gary's sisters. Her message read, "I feel Gary wants you to feel comfort and know everything is alright. She has no limitations where she is now. My prayers are with you."

She also told me that she believed that because Stephanie had left us on the eve of Gary's birthday, eight months to the day after his death that Gary was there to welcome her. His family believed Stephanie was with him. I got the confirmation I had asked for. I still wanted more.

Not too long after the funeral, a friend visited and spent the night at my house. I had gone to bed while my friend stayed up watching a movie in the living room. The next morning she told me that she saw a shadow out of the corner of her eye walking around the kitchen the night before. She described a shadow that was about the same height as Stephanie. She did not see any facial features but there was a human form. She said the shadow went from Stephanie's chair over to the refrigerator then back to the chair. Kathryn did not typically see apparitions. This was a completely new experience for her and she found it quite disturbing. Like my older daughter, she was not one who subscribed to paranormal activity, so an unlikely candidate to fabricate such an encounter.

Eventually all of the dreams and signs tapered off. Not seeing my child on a regular basis was unbearable. Never having really gotten the type of visitation I expected and needed, I yearned for more. Most people would question at this point, what exactly was I expecting? The issue is that with the grief of losing a child, it is so profound that we become very irrational. Also when a parent grieves for a child, we want the child just like it was when they were alive, in our lives every day. My expectations were unrealistic due to grief.

My therapist suggested that I had not gotten the sign I wanted because I had not formally said good-bye to my daughter. I had no chance to say good-bye. Stephanie died very quickly in her sleep. I had just talked to her twenty minutes earlier and she had been fine. There was no indication that she would disappear from this world so suddenly. When death is sudden, there is a certain relief that our loved one felt no pain, no fear. But it also denies us the opportunity for preparation for the loss. There is no time for good-bye. Sudden unexpected death, even in a child that suffered a sickly childhood, can take a parent by surprise causing tremendous shock and grief. The effects of such a shock can cause post-traumatic stress disorder that lingers for years. For a parent who has lost a child, PTSD causes the parent to relive that child's last moments again and again. It can be sheer torture to a parent. But if one believes in an afterlife, is goodbye really necessary? I went through elaborate rituals to say good-bye to my daughter.

I decorated her grave. I made a memorial garden in the front garden under her bedroom window. I created an altar of her favorite things on her dresser. I cleaned her closet and her room. I attended a butterfly release that the Compassionate Friends held. I also had purchased a brick with Stephanie's name on it for the children's garden at the local park through Compassionate Friends. I invited friends and family to attend the dedication. It was quite a sendoff for her. This was almost three months after her very formal elaborate funeral that included an open casket wake the evening before, and a full Catholic mass before the burial. Her name was carved into the family headstone and a small angel statue added to the gravesite. I felt like I had said good-bye to her over and over again. I still did not have the sign I wanted and that was to see her face to face and hear her tell me that she was fine and in a good place.

In the process of saying goodbye I did have a couple of dreams of her. But in none of them did she communicate. In the first two dreams, she was an infant. In the first dream, I was riding the street car looking for her. When I found her, she was a tiny infant. She was alive and fine but an infant. I found her and picked her up, safe in my arms; then I woke up. In the second dream, I found her on a large set of steps which resembled a scene from the movie, *What Dreams May Come*. She was in an infant seat. Her face was blank and her eyes glazed. I feared she was dead so I screamed out her name. She jumped as if startled by my cry. Then she smiled. I took her out of the seat and carried her off. But again, she was an infant. She could not walk, nor talk, only smile as a reaction. I wondered what the dream meant. But I knew that it was merely my subconscious working out my issues with the loss. It was not a visitation dream. Perhaps my search for her provoked these dreams. I definitely did not consider either of these confirmations that she was alright.

The third dream came a few weeks later. She was an adult but again did not speak in the dream. She was dressed in hospital gown and we were in the hospital. I kissed her forehead and hugged her then we went through a set of double doors that led to some strange medical room. The room was dark and I could not see into it. Figures in white met her down a long hallway and she was escorted away. I left her there knowing, I would never see her again. I walked back through the double doors feeling sad and empty. Again, this was hardly a comforting dream of confirmation that my child's spirit lived on. Rather, I felt that this dream represented my saying goodbye to her.

I thought of the profound messages I had gotten from Gary. The words he told me in the dream after he died turned over in my head, "Everything happens exactly the way it is supposed to."

As the dreams stopped and my daughter seemed to be gone completely from my life, I began to seek out other methods of communication in a desperate attempt to continue contact with her.

Chapter Nine
Remembering

"For life and death are one, even as the river and the sea are one." ~ Khalil Gibran

Death was nothing foreign to me. My parents were well into mid-life when I was born. It seemed that throughout my entire life, there was always somebody having a funeral. My parents were very respectful of the dead and death customs, but at the same time, very matter of fact about it all. We were very traditional old school Catholics. I had been taught that life continued after death. You died, you were judged, and you went to heaven or hell. Purgatory was an in between place for those who weren't quite ready for heaven but weren't horrible enough to be condemned to hell. Limbo was a different place, specifically for unbaptized babies.

When someone died in my family, there was the traditional evening wake on the night before the mass and burial. Most wakes were open casket, unless the body was severely damaged from an accident. Visitation of the deceased was considered a must. This gave everyone an opportunity to say good-bye. No one in the family explained much about grieving. Although some tears were shed at the wake, mass, and funeral, very little was ever discussed or explained. The tone of the wake period was solemn and quiet. Family members gathered together to support each other at the time of bereavement. The immediate family was brought food by others so they would not have to cook or concern themselves with daily chores. The following morning, a full Catholic mass was held with the coffin at the church.

After the mass, the casket was transported to the cemetery, where it would be interned into a gravesite, mausoleum, or tomb. In New Orleans, the above could be shared by all the family members. The state requires that a year and a day must pass before another coffin can be interned in a family vault or plot. The remains in the coffin can be emptied into the grave or vault and the used coffin is thrown away. The space is now cleared for a new coffin to enter. This is why in New Orleans cemeteries, headstones have several names of family members engraved onto them.

After the funeral, a big party was held at the home of a family member. There were no obvious tears at the party. It was time to celebrate the life of the deceased loved one. I always thought it was strange how people could be so sorrowful one minute, then chatting and even laughing moments later. It always seemed odd to me as a child. I understood the concept of celebrating the life of the deceased. The point, of course, is to remember the good times. It hardly prepares one for the reality of dealing with massive loss, such as when a child dies.

I found this part very difficult after my daughter's funeral. I had not even adjusted to the loss and properly grieved for her, much less ready to celebrate for her. I was merely going through the motions. In the beginning, I made many trips to the cemetery. It was as if I could not stay away.

Honoring the dead was important to my family. My parents were constantly tending to the gravesites and bringing flowers to honor the dead ancestors. Visitations to the cemetery throughout the year, and masses said for the souls of the deceased, were common in my family. This became agonizing for me, seeing her grave, knowing she was in the ground.

Death and death rituals were considered to be a normal part of the cycle of life. Despite my family's healthy attitude toward death, and so many deaths surrounding my life very early on, I was never present for anyone who had died. Both of my parents died in the hospital, and they did it when I had my back turned.

My father was diagnosed with emphysema when he was seventy-years-old. He also suffered from dementia, caused from atherosclerosis (hardening of the arteries) and vascular dementia. I was eighteen when he died. I remember him spending time in the hospital and dying there, but not much else.

Before any procedures could be performed that might have helped his conditions, he was taken from this world suddenly by a blood clot to the lung. He died instantly. The family felt that he was spared any long term suffering and lingering. He died while the entire family was not present. My mother never quite got over the loss. She died two years later from a stroke. She had a multitude of health issues, including diabetes and high blood pressure. She had suffered a mild stroke and been hospitalized for it. Just a few days later, she suffered a massive stroke that killed her. I was just arriving at the hospital as the staff was leaving the room with machines to attempt to resuscitate her.

In both cases, I never got to say good-bye to them. It was not until many years later, as I mourned for my daughter, that I realized how I never truly allowed myself to grieve their deaths. I handled both situations as I was taught; quietly, and with dignity, moving forward immediately into my own life. It was only now that I was beginning to understand how much I had pushed it away from my awareness. I tried to remember details surrounding their deaths and could not. I had very few memories of either of their funeral services or anything that happened during that period of time. I was beginning to realize that I had never mourned the loss of my parents. Once my parents were gone, many years went by before I had to deal with death again. Whenever a relative passed away, I would slip into avoidance and send my condolences; never attending any formal services. I got by like this for many years. The few services I did attend, I did only physically. My mind would zone out and drift somewhere else, never really dealing with feelings of the loss. I had become an expert at avoidance.

Even when my brother died, I did not face his death head on. My brother and I were very close, despite the fact that there was a twenty-four year difference in our ages. He died when he was seventy-four-years-old of lung cancer. Once again, someone I loved died when I was not present. As with my parents, I received a phone call informing me of his passing.

In retrospect, one of the things that helped me in all of the cases of loss was that I had my children to think about. I had to be strong for them. I had to keep my wits about me to take care of them. Even though when my brother died, my oldest daughter was grown up, I still had Stephanie, who needed me in my right mind. It was easy for me to justify their deaths because of their age as well. I could be sad but still be thankful that they had lived good lives, and although I would have wished them to live longer, they were old enough to understand that deaths were normal processes that were to be expected. It was easy for me to make excuses for falling so easily into acceptance.

When I volunteered at Project Lazarus House as a student, I became physically ill because of my unresolved issues with death. I walked around with an aura of heaviness surrounding me. When I would arrive at the house, I would feel knots in my stomach. I dreaded going in to see who had died the night before. I was never in attendance when anyone actually died. I could not handle it. I tried to face my fears at the time and simply could not. They begged me stay on after my service hours were complete, but I couldn't take it. It disturbed me to be so close to the dying. I pushed it out of my life and out of my awareness and moved forward, denying it.

In 2012, several people, whom I had known well, died. One of which was a very good friend, Gary. His death came early at only fifty-six. This was the first time since my childhood death had hit so close to home. I was in my early teens the last time death called upon someone in my inner circle. When I was a teenager, I knew several kids that had died. A neighbor's baby died of meningitis when he was only a year old. Shortly after that, a little girl that my family knew died from Reye's syndrome. A boy that was part of my teenage click also died, from a sudden case of encephalitis. As a teenager, I recall being sad and traumatized by the losses, but blocked it from my conscious mind over time. I tried to apply my normal diplomacy in handling his death, but each time fell back into deep sadness, unable to accept that Gary was gone. This time it was too close to home to deny. The only thing that gave me solace was that he had said goodbye, and I did get messages from him immediately. For some reason, he seemed to have a direct line of communication that I did not have with my family members or other people that had died during my life.

When I attended his wake the night before his burial, I stood in a long line of people walking up to pay their respects to the open casket and the family. He was quite famous, so there were people from all over who came for the visitation. As I approached the casket, I saw his body lying inside and my knees got weak. I looked away and saw his favorite vest and guitar on a chair nearby. I felt as if I would fall over. Suddenly, I felt his presence with me. It was as if he was standing behind me looking over my shoulder.

He whispered, "Kat, it's not me in there, just my body. I'm here, behind you. It's okay."

Even with all of the confirmations and messages that I received from him, several months after his death, I eventually found myself pushing him aside, too. I would break down every time I listened to his music; so I stopped listening to it. I told others that I didn't have time to be depressed, so I just shut down and pushed all the sadness down inside of me, denying its existence.

When my daughter died only eight months later, there was nowhere to hide. Grief hit me like an angry storm ravaging everything in its path. The last time I saw her she was in her bed unresponsive, waiting for the ambulance to arrive. Nothing I had ever experienced in my life had prepared me to face this loss. My mind and body became victim to grief and its devastating effects.

My mother often spoke of her brother who had died as a small child. She never mentioned how her mother, my grandmother, handled the loss. In the following months as I faced my grief and worked my way through it, I began to realize all of the times I had denied my grieving process. I grieved for them all as I grieved for my daughter. My sorrow was so dense that I missed many of the signs that were in front of my face all along.

I became a victim of my own uncontrolled emotions. By the end of the third month, I was drowning in despair. I had lost all faith in everything. I felt hopeless. What little that was left inside of me was also dying. I dug deeper in a desperate attempt to find something to give me hope that one day, I would see my precious child again.

Once I allowed grief to flow, it was an unstoppable force. I had no control over it. It controlled me. I did not awaken on any given day and decide that I would feel sad or angry, it just happened, without warning. During this time, I faced my feelings directly. I read books on grief, attended group meetings and one-on-one therapy sessions to release the emotions.

I had studied emotional release therapy and was more aware than most people of the negative effects of holding emotions inside the body. I utilized all I had in my memories of the body-mind techniques, Gestalt, and NLP to help pull the emotions out and experience them, no matter how painful.

As I worked out my grief and wrote a book to help not only myself but hopefully others as well, I continued to find answers on the afterlife. Somewhere in my grief, I had lost faith in everything I had once believed. I questioned all of my own research on life continuing after death, as well as my religious upbringing. I discussed with friends my fears and insecurities, all the while feeling as if I was losing my mind.

I was so consumed with grief that I could not see a way out. I was blinded by grief. I could not see that I was so consumed with negative emotions that I was unable to allow any spiritual experiences in. I mentioned to one friend, who is very spiritual, of my concerns and her only response was, "You either have faith or you don't; there is no in between."

Not understanding where I was in my grieving process left her unable to empathize and offer advice. I certainly couldn't see any answers in my pathetic emotional state.

I talked to another friend, Phillip, who was a psychic/medium that had worked with me for years on various investigations. He said to me, "You know the things we've experienced over the years were real. You know this."

"Do I?" I asked, "Did we just imagine it; make it all up?"

"No," he insisted.

"I don't know what I believe any more, if anything at all," I told him.

"Usually when that happens, eventually you find something new to believe in," he responded.

It reminded me of the former director of the Gestalt Institute of New Orleans, Anne Teachworth, who had also died within the past year. If a client would say to her that he was confused, she would always respond, *"Good! I love confusion."*

In Gestalt therapy, confusion is the first step in change and in awareness. It made sense to me.

"I just feel like I'm losing my mind," I said, "and I have no faith in anything."

"Well, that's not good," he said, "without faith, there's no hope."

One morning as I pulled my tired, aching body from yet another restless night in bed, I called a friend who was an RN, and discussed my physical ailments. She explained that the aches, the pains, the weight gain, and the sleeplessness were all full blown depression. I had gotten past the panic attacks that plagued me in the beginning phases, and the high blood pressure, but now was feeling the effects of depression on my body. I couldn't concentrate. Every movement, every thought, every breath was difficult for me.

I felt hopeless. I darted from one book to another not realizing that I had become my own worst enemy. My breaking point came finally one weekend when I had taken several days off to get some things done around the house.

With no work to do, nowhere to be, all alone, I was forced to face my worst enemy; myself.

As I attempted to accomplish something productive, I found myself becoming more and more distracted. I was unable to focus on any one thing. I didn't have the energy to go outside and attempt yard work. I stared blankly at the computer in an attempt to write. Before I knew it, I was in the bathroom crying hysterically, unable to stop. The only thought that kept going through my mind was "I cannot do this. I can't live without her."

I was crying so hard I couldn't stand up. I could hardly breathe. There was no game plan; I just doubled over with a crying fit unable to find any solace. A friend called breaking my sobbing spell. I caught my breath, explaining to her how I did not know what to do any more. I just knew I couldn't handle this tragedy that had been thrown upon me.

As I talked to her, I poured myself a glass of wine, which served to calm my hysteria. I stayed up reading various web sites still searching for something; anything that would stop the pain. Nothing did. The gaping wound that was once my heart ached for my daughter. I dragged myself through each day, feeling lost and alone, with nothing but despair within my reach.

The anticipatory response to the upcoming four-month anniversary of my daughter's death, along with the year anniversary of Gary's death, was hitting me hard. My emotions and body reacted out of my control at the upcoming dreadful anniversaries. I felt as if I was losing what little sanity I had left. My world was becoming a dark and scary place. My only peace was what little sleep I would get. I rarely dreamed, and if I did, I did not remember anything. My dreamless sleep was but brief moments of respite in the agony of what had become my life. I wondered why I was left here in this world alone to experience this pain. My pain was all I could see.

A few days later I began to see signs from Gary, as mentioned in earlier chapters that distracted me from my pain. No longer could I deny what I was seeing, as others noticed them, too. This was hardly my imagination. Things like the heron that was seen by everyone in my tour group. It was completely out of place and met the criteria that Dr. Moody had described in several of his books. When the bird appeared again a half of block from my home on the twenty-fifth of May, the exact anniversary date, there was no mistake. I wished in hindsight that I had thought to photograph it. I was so emotional that the thought did not occur to me either time that the bird was seen. One night after the heron had appeared the first time, the dragonfly appeared on my door. I began to feel a glimmer of hope that maybe, those who had been loved and lost still existed somewhere and they were trying to reach out to me.

It was also during this time that I had run into a local psychic, who invited me to a nearby metaphysical fair. Little did I know at the time, the door that would be opened to the other side through this innocuous encounter. My world and my viewpoint would soon change dramatically in just one afternoon with a local medium.

Chapter Ten
Messages

"I've told my children that when I die, to release balloons in the sky to celebrate that I graduated. For me, death is a graduation." ~ Elisabeth Kubler-Ross

There is a very strong case in favor of life continuing after death. From the dawn of time, every civilization and culture had a belief in the afterlife. Recently, a Neanderthal burial ground was found in Southern Spain. These early humans buried their dead with flowers. It is unknown the intention of these people, but it could be indicative of showing respect and honor to their deceased.

In *Searching for Spirits*, I examined the history of humankind's obsession with the afterlife. Most early civilizations had specific burial procedures to ensure safe passageway to another life. Early civilizations built great tombs and temples to pay homage to the dead. The ancient Egyptians buried their dead with treasures. Servants were often killed and buried along with them to continue to serve kings in the afterlife. Ancient religions always included gods and goddesses who ruled the spirit world. In addition to a belief in an afterlife, most of these civilizations also believed in communication with those who have crossed over.

During the Victorian Era, the séance became very popular. Americans and Europeans alike used mediums to channel the spirits of deceased loved ones. Although many of the mediums of that era turned out to be charlatans, fascination with contacting the dead continued through the ages.

The networks are flooded with television shows that revolve

around communicating with spirits. They range from those who *hunt* ghosts, capturing voices on recorders, to mediums who claim to make direct contact with loved ones. We all want to know where our loved ones have gone and where we will go when our time is up. It was my own curiosity and fear of death that provoked me to spend the past almost twenty years researching the other side.

Having had experiences and communication with spirits throughout my life, I felt that through my research and writing I had pretty much answered all of my own questions about life after death. I was content in my beliefs until my daughter's death turned my world upside down. Everything I believed was now challenged. In hindsight, I realize that at the time, I also overreacted to everything. Every molehill was transformed into a mountain. If I read a half of sentence that came from a skeptical perspective, something I might have ignored before would catapult me into hysteria. Grief makes no sense. The chemical reaction going on inside the brain, and the rest of the body, is so overwhelming that it turns a once rational individual into a histrionic mess.

When Stephanie died, the bond that was broken caused so much pain that I was not able to rationalize any of my own beliefs. A part of me was severed and I wanted nothing short of having her back, which was not possible. It didn't matter what I had believed in the past. I had to relearn and reprove everything to myself from scratch, little by little.

The television mediums were bombarded with bereaved people like me on a continual basis. Desperate, grief-stricken people who need someone to prove to them that their loved ones are still nearby. We all require this kind of validation at some point in time.

Sometimes, messages come via a third party who is not a medium, or even aware that they are being used as messengers. Shortly after Stephanie died, I was sitting at my desk feeling awful. I missed her so much and wanted to know if she was alright. I began to cry and talk to her. I told her that I wished I knew that she was okay. Then the phone rang.

When I answered a young woman asked for me by my maiden name from high school.

She then said, "You probably don't remember me; it's Sarah, Paula's daughter."

Paula was a woman with whom I had gone to high school with over thirty years ago. She later became a special education teacher at Stephanie's school. Stephanie adored Paula and had been deeply affected when she passed away the year before.

The first question Sarah asked me was, "How is Stephanie?"

Obviously she had not called to give her condolences. I informed her of Stephanie's death and she was deeply saddened. She then asked me about another student her mother and I had known from years before. During the course of the conversation and after, I realized that Sarah was in touch with several other people on a social network that she could have easily contacted, yet she took the steps to look up my business phone number and trace me to ask me. I felt as if this perhaps was a message from Paula telling me that Stephanie was okay. I called another high school friend, Bobbi, and told her what had happened. She got chills when I shared the story. She too felt it was a message from Paula.

With the emergence of mass communication, more and more people are able to share stories of communication with their loved ones. What was once considered occult activity is now accepted as mainstream. Even the Catholic Church has become more accepting of receiving messages from the other side.

In a 1999 interview for the London Observer Service, journalist John Hooper wrote an article that later posted on www.after-death.com, the website owned by Bill and Judy Guggenheim:

One of the most authoritative spokesmen of the Roman Catholic Church has raised eyebrows among the faithful by declaring that the Church believes in the feasibility of communication with the dead.

Kalila Smith with Stephanie Link

The Rev. Gino Concetti, chief theological commentator for the Vatican newspaper, L'Osservatore Romano, denied he was signaling any change in approach. But he agreed that his remarks might come as a jolt to many believers.

He said the Church remained opposed to the raising of spirits, but added: "Communication is possible between those who live on this earth and those who live in a state of eternal repose, in heaven or purgatory. It may even be that God lets our loved ones send us messages to guide us at certain moments in our life."

His comments were first made in support of an American theologian, the Rev. John Neuhaus. Neuhaus had described how a friend had seen a ghost. He said there were various explanations, but "the important thing is not to deny such things a priority."

Concetti said the key to the Church's attitude was the Roman Catholic belief in a "Communion of Saints," which included Christians on earth as well as those in the after-life. "Where there is communion, there is communication," he said.

Concetti suggested dead relatives could be responsible for prompting impulses and triggering inspiration - and even for "sensory manifestations," such as appearances in dreams.

Concetti said the new Catholic catechism specifically endorsed the view that the dead could intercede on earth and quotes the dying St. Dominic telling his brothers: "Do not weep, for I shall be more useful to you after my death and I shall help you then more effectively than during my life."

This is a major shift in the Church's thinking. Having grown up in the Church, I was taught that all communication with the dead was considered dangerous. Albeit I understand their stand on this issue; one cannot be one hundred percent certain that messages are coming from deceased loved one and not an evil entity. This is why I so easily became skeptical of everything I had experienced. I was not certain that is was coming from my daughter. I needed more specific messages to be sure. It is very important and great take needs to be taken to ensure that the spirit coming through is indeed the deceased loved ones. Evil entities can be extremely deceiving.

Friends in the spiritual community warned me not to attempt to force communication with her because of that very reason. While I do believe that there are evil ones that set out to deceive and trick, I also believe that some communication is direct from our loved ones. When my friend appeared to me and told me good-bye then returned to tell me that he was okay, this was not a demon. There was nothing said that encouraged me to be depressed or continue on a road of negative emotions or actions. It was comforting and gave me peace.

But there had been no peace since I lost my daughter. My brain was so jumbled from stress that I could barely make rational decisions about anything. I had been trying to decide for days if I was going to take a trip to Mobile for the weekend, and just could not decide if I wanted to go or not.

I walked up to the corner of Royal Street and St. Peter Street, and as I walked by Rouse's grocery store, a local psychic, whom I've known for year, Jen, was walking out. I said hello and she immediately gave me her condolences on my loss. She then told me about a metaphysical fair that took place every other month and the next one was happening in a couple of days. She also recommended a particular psychic named Nicole.

Finally a decision was made for me. There would be no trip to Mobile when there was something interesting that might give me answers right here in my own backyard. Two days later, I was at the metaphysical fair.

I walked around the fair looking at various tables and talking to a variety of people. I sat down with Nicole who started her reading off with a prayer. She explained that she tuned into the Holy Spirit for guidance. Amazingly she began to discuss things about me that she could not have possibly known. Not only did she tune into my plans for a book and counseling work, but also she somehow knew that my vehicle had been broken down for a while, and that I had borrowed a car from my ex-husband. This was something I considered to be very incidental and not a major focal point in my life, but I took it as confirmation that she really was tuning into issues in my life.

She then turned her attention to my daughter. She explained to me that another spirit, an unidentified guide was speaking, not Stephanie herself. The guide explained that it was time for Stephanie to work on the other side. The guide also told Nicole that it was time for me to do specific work that could not be done in this world if Stephanie stayed. It was explained that we all have work that needs to be completed and mine was to be done here. I needed to move in another direction. Stephanie's work was now on the other side. She was finished here. This was the second time that I had gotten this type of message from spirit. Both times it was not just that she is some beautiful place but specifically that she had spiritual work, too, and it involved helping others evolve.

A month before this particular reading, I attended a spiritual misa, which is a Santerian mass for the dead; often called a séance. Unlike the séances of Victorian era, these are based on the séances conducted by Allan Kardec. Kardec was a pen name for Hippolyte Léon Denizard Rivail, a French educator who wrote numerous books on spiritism in the mid-1800s. Kardec developed a system for communicating with spirits based on what he describes as a science of communication between the living and the dead; spiritism. His principals are based on the teaching of Jesus while adding the dimension of spiritual evolution through reincarnation, an Eastern philosophy.

The traditional Kardecian séance became very popular in Brazil and other Caribbean countries. It is often incorporated in various Afro-Caribbean religious sects such as Santeria. The purpose of the misa is to learn to develop one's ability to know when messages from spirit are being delivered. I happen to attend these misas on a regular basis.

One such occasion, I was told by someone during a misa the

same message given to me by Nicole.

Shortly after Stephanie's death, I attended a misa in hopes of getting messages from her. During the session, one of the participants informed me that he was getting a vision of my daughter, and she was in a beautiful garden. She was not alone. It was during this session that I received my second confirmation that Stephanie was with Gary.

A participant in the session asked, "Do you know a gentleman who plays acoustic guitar?"

I naturally said that I did, knowing he was seeing Gary. He went on to describe to me that the two of them were sitting in a garden together singing songs and laughing. The message that Gary sent via this person was that Stephanie and he were both fine and that they hoped I would be able to find my peace, even though I was left here without my daughter.

Another participant spoke, "You need to become that carefree girl you used to be."

Later after the misa, my godfather spoke to me, knowing I was in so much pain. He told me that he had heard from someone in our Santos house in Miami who explained that usually when people died in this tradition, we pray that their spirit be elevated. According to this Santera, it was not necessary in Stephanie's case. Everyone agreed that because she was mentally handicapped, her spirit was already elevated. In Santeria, as in many religions, these children are considered sacred to God and their spirits go directly to be with God. They believed that she was already enlightened.

He warned me not to allow my sorrow to bind her to this physical plane hindering her ability to ascend to her fullest potential. Sometimes in our sorrow, we bind our loved ones spirits to the physical, and prevent them from evolving. Negative emotions can bind them to the physical plane, and this is never anything we should intentionally do. I tried desperately to let Stephanie go and allow her to ascend. Even though I wished for my daughter's spirit to be at rest and to ascend to God's presence, I could not control the range of emotions that controlled me.

When I talked to Nicole everything that had been said two

months before at this misa was verified. It was a small step for me but I was able to believe what messages I had received thus far and felt somewhat comforted by them. I was beginning to heal.

I still needed more proof. I made an appointment to have a one on one session with a local medium, Sid Patrick, the following Monday. The real answers were soon to come even though at the time, I remained skeptical. I left no stone unturned. I figured at best, I'd get a message that I knew was from my daughter, at worst, I'd have a story to tell of my disappointment. When you desperately want to communicate with a loved one on the other side, you'll give anything a shot. I was very desperate at this point.

A medium is a person who is able to mediate communication between spirits and the living. Unlike a clairvoyant, the medium does not necessarily see future events or make predictions. What the medium does is bring messages from the other side to loved ones who are eager to know if their deceased friend or family member still exists.

In my book *Searching for Spirits: The Ultimate Guide for Ghost Hunters*, I discussed the mediums of the 19th century:

In the Victorian era, Europeans and Americans alike cultivated an obsession with spiritualism, communication with the dead. During the Victorian Era, obsession with death turned into fashion as communication with the dead became a favorite past time as well as a dark form of entertainment. In "The History of Spiritualism," by Arthur Conan Doyle, the first spiritualist, Emanuel Swedenborg (1688-1772) was outlined. Swedenborg was the first European to popularize the idea that communication was possible with spiritual beings other than those of a higher order. He was the first to note that there were various planes to the spirit realm.

Clairvoyant, Andrew Jackson Davis (1826-1910), is accredited with the father of Modern Spiritualism. He became interested in mesmerism (hypnotism) and through attending seminars on the subject discovered that in a trance state could diagnose medical disorders in others. Through his mind's eye in an altered state, he could literally see through the physical body and directly at organs inside.

In 1844, he experienced an out of body trance state and found himself 40 miles away in the Catskills Mountains. It was there that he envisioned the apparitions of the philosopher Galen and the Swedish seer Emanuel Swedenborg, both of whom were dead. This bizarre experience had a great impact on Davis. He began to travel giving lectures on the subject of spiritualism. It was through these travels that he met Dr. Lyons and Rev. Fishboug. Dr. Lyons was a renowned mesmerist who began a series of trance sessions on Davis. In the trance state, Davis dictated "The Principles of Nature: Her Divine Revelations and A Voice To Mankind." The process took fifteen months to complete. Due to his lack of education, it is presumed that Davis was truly channeling from a higher source, perhaps even Swedenborg himself. "Principles of Nature" was published in 1847. He went on to write over 30 books on the subject. He eventually obtained a medical degree and retired in Boston.

It was also in the latter part of the eighteenth century that Madame Helen P. Blavatsky began her teachings on Theosophy. The word translated from Greek to mean "Divine Wisdom." The principles of Theosophy dealt with the unity of life, the law of cycles, and the progressive consciousness in all kingdoms of nature (both visible and invisible). Madame Blavatsky taught of the origin and development of the universe and the origin and evolution of humanity. She taught of the nature (spiritual and psychological) of humans and of life after death.

After almost twenty years of research, writing, and teaching about these principals, I was about to put them to test. Like Houdini, who in the early twentieth century became obsessed with communicating with his deceased mother, I was obsessed with exploring as many ways possible to reach my daughter.

Chapter Eleven
Finally, Contact!

"I am well aware that many will say that no one can possibly speak with spirits and angels so long as he lives in the body; and many will say that it is all fancy, others that I relate such things in order to gain credence, and others will make other objections." ~ Emanuel Swedenborg

Medium Sid Patrick was the organizer of the metaphysical event I had attended. Prior to the weekend, I arranged to have a private reading with him. I had looked up his biography on the internet and was pretty impressed. He was raised in Metairie, right outside of New Orleans. His aunt read playing cards but limited her readings to only *certain people*.

Sid always had a connection to the spirit world throughout his entire life. He began reading tarot cards at only thirteen. Even at such an early age, he knew that he had a special gift. He worked with NOPD on murder cases, missing persons and pets, conducted spiritual cleansings on houses, and worked on numerous television shows and events.

Like many of us, he began to really involve himself with the afterlife questions when he lost his mother. Like me, his grief drove him further into seeking answers to questions about life after death.

He took many developmental classes under psychic Louise Decker. He studied under many others in Sedona, Arizona, a Spiritualist Camp in Indiana, and in England. He had travelled the world to a variety of spiritual places as he attuned himself to the spirit world.

Kalila Smith with Stephanie Link

The day before my session with Sid, I had experienced a complete emotional breakdown. I was at rock bottom with depression and hopelessness. I didn't believe anything anymore. I had been tempted to cancel my appointment, assuming all was lost, so why even try? But for some reason, I had not cancelled. I tried in vain to walk into the appointment at the very least with a neutral attitude. I definitely had no expectations. I pulled in front of the suburban house a few minutes early and sat in the car for a moment trying to ground myself a bit. I reluctantly walked up to the front door. I was met by a pleasant gentleman, who escorted me into a waiting area, and asked me to be seated. He explained that the Sid was still in another appointment and would be available shortly. Sid was with a client and I could hear him apologizing to her. He was explaining how not everyone can tune in every time.

Doing what I do, I understood what he was talking about and thought to myself, "Well, at least he's honest and not just out for the buck obviously."

I began to relax, seeing that he was not merely saying what the client wanted to hear. In fact, she was a bit upset. I would rather see a psychic or medium with an unhappy client that he did not charge, then slop through a reading or session, saying what he thought the client wanted to hear. It was at this point that I knew that he was sincere and took pride in what he did.

After his other client left, a frazzled Sid Patrick entered the room to greet me. He attempted to explain the situation. I told him that I understood completely. When a client shows up late then has a time limit rushing the medium, it creates a stressful situation that would make it difficult for anyone to pick up on anything. He assured me that if he picked up nothing, I owed him nothing.

"It doesn't get any fairer than that," I told him.

We moved to the other room and began the session. Immediately, Sid began to get a vision. He said he felt sadness and something I had not resolved yet. He explained up front that when I added him to my Face Book, he saw the profile photo of my daughter and me. He said at that time she stepped forward and he had hoped it was not her. He also indicated that he was seeing her again. He asked, "Is this your daughter?"

I told him that she was. I knew that he did not know anything beyond that from my profile, since I had restricted him on my profile. He was only able to see general posts I made public.

He then asked, "Is your daughter still with us…here?"

"No, she is not," I answered.

"I was hoping that was not the case," he said.

He continued, "She is here….no wait, there is also someone else. There is a male and a female; they're both coming at me. They travel together."

At this point, I already knew where this was going. He was going to tell me that she was with Gary. This was the third or fourth confirmation that those two were together on the other side. I settled into my chair and took a deep breath. I went from complete loss of belief to believer immediately. I listened as Sid described what was going on beyond the veil.

"They are arguing over who gets to talk first," he said.

"She said she's first, then he says, no it's me," he told me.

He then said, "He's winning."

"He always does," I said.

I knew Gary had stepped forward and he had been with Steph all these months.

Sid paced back and forth as he gave me a vivid description of Gary. I sat quietly answering "*yes*," as he asked questions relating to identifying him.

He's kind of sassy. He always has a good comeback. I agreed. Sid said, "He gives me goose bumps, and he definitely gave them to you. He's very playful."

Sid continued to describe the man and without a doubt, it was Gary.

He told me that Gary was very protective of Stephanie. "Oh, she's saying a bit too over protective," he added.

Sid gave accurate details on messages that could only come from Gary. He said that Gary told him that I would walk through a large doorway with three circles or full moons across the top and this would be a sign for me to know that it was really him coming through. I already knew though. When Sid described him as having died because of an *obstruction to breathing*, I knew. Gary had died from obstructive sleep apnea. Sid was the real deal. There is no way he could have possibly had the information and details that he was giving to me. He was definitely getting messages directly from Gary. Sid explained that both of them liked to hang out together.

He went on to say that the man was telling him something about religion. He asked, "Was there a difference in religious beliefs?"

"Yes, and no, I know what that means," I said.

Gary and I had both been raised very traditional Catholics. But I had ventured down the roads of Voodoo and Santeria. To me, they were all very much in line with one another. To him, they were not. He had expressed throughout time to me that he did not like my affiliation with other religions that were not Catholic. My family would have agreed. I never really thought it was a problem. But here it was a topic of argument once again, this time from the other side.

Sid told me, "She's saying 'Mom, you know I'm with you,' the little clues that you get are coming from her."

Sid suddenly laughed. He said, "He just told me 'how dare you tell her that I don't communicate.'"

Sid said "You need to know that they are together and that she is protected."

He then said to Gary, "I want you to step back and let her talk."

Sid said, "She is saying, 'I want to talk to my mother for one minute. Mom, you were the most positive thing in my life.'"

Sid continued, "She's saying that she chose you as her mother. And she thanks you for all you gave her. You gave her opportunities that so many mothers might not have done. She is thanking you for letting her get involved in life. She wants to tell you that she is okay and she knows that you constantly worry about her. She says, 'Mom, I'm just a shout away.'"

Sid went on, "She's fine. She wants you to be able to move on but not forget her, but move on and release the emotions and then she will be able to get closer to you."

He described our connection to the spirit world like a big piece of cellophane that is stretched across the two worlds, dividing them. They can see and hear us and we cannot always see and hear them. They try to push through that cellophane to reach you.

"Imagine how frustrating it is for spirits when they are trying to communicate," he told me.

"She does come through but she feels like you don't pay attention, so I need you to pay attention," he said.

He then explained that the hold-up in receiving messages from her was my grieving process. It was preventing me from hearing and seeing messages from the other side.

He went on, "I know you know Kubler-Ross and all the others and could probably spit it at me verbatim. They are telling me you know. But you're stuck in the grief process. You will never lose the connection with your daughter. Once she feels you are able to handle her presence, she's going to come. She knows you are not ready. You need to work with letting go of the pain so she can communicate with you. Spirits are not going to do anything that is going to put us in a state that is not healthy for us. She doesn't want you to go back she wants you to move forward."

Stephanie also told Sid that she did not know why she died. She was aware that it was quick but had no idea what had happened to her. He said that Stephanie feels bad about leaving abruptly, but on the other side, she really cannot feel bad. He explains that it's different there. She told Sid that she is with me all the time. She feels that she is still here, just as she was always still on the other side a great deal. She always walked in both worlds and still does.

There was no way Sid could have known all of these fine details. I was so blown away by the communication I sat there dumbfounded. I was surprised that she was again with Gary. I knew he had to be connected to them both to get these details.

She said that I need to heal before she can get through to me. Sid then saw a face of a reindeer, like a Christmas picture. She had died exactly one month after Christmas and had colored a reindeer picture. He then said that she wanted me to "spread my wings and share the love that I had with the world."

She said, "I need my mom to move forward with projects that have been put aside. The more she moves forward the closer I can get to her."

Before the session ended, Sid said that Gary said to get my sense of humor back and when I see a green feather, I'll know I have it. Sid also reminded me to keep an eye out for the doorway with the three moons or circles on it.

That night I fell into a deep sleep. I found myself walking in a beautiful field. I could feel the sunlight on my skin and the cool breeze on my face and in my hair. I could smell the flowers and sweet grass that blew gently in the breeze. I could hear birds and insects nearby. Suddenly, Gary was walking beside me. He was dressed in the white linen shirt again. He was laughing and hugging me.

"You know that was me, right?" he laughed.

"Yes, I do," I answered.

"I told you to trust me, everything was alright, you know that now," he kept laughing.

"Where is Steph?" I asked him.

He then got very serious, he said, "Kat, she's got a lot to do. She's learning things. Just like you have things to do there, she has things to do here."

It was then that not only did I realize that the session with Sid was very real, but the message from Stephanie now made sense. She said move forward. She meant to evolve spiritually. That is what she was doing and she needed me to do the same thing here. She was encouraging me to evolve to a higher place in my spiritual awareness as she evolved in spirit.

I told Gary that I understood what she was dealing with. He gave me another hug and his laughter drifted away as I awakened back in my bed. I know that dream was real. I have severe insomnia and rarely sleep deep enough to dream, much less remember my dreams. Without a doubt now, I knew that all of my communication with both Gary and Steph had been real experiences. Knowing that she was safe and still existed gave me great comfort. Knowing that they were together was even more comforting. They had not simply ceased to exist. I had not imagined my experiences, it was all very, very real. The afterlife was real. I still missed both of them but now I could at least heal with the knowledge that one day I would reunite with them both. They would wait for me and be there when I arrived. I felt sure of this now. Both of them gave specific advice on advancing spiritually. I did not take those messages lightly. Obviously where they were, they knew and could see things more clearly than I could here. I had to pay attention to these messages. The one thing I knew for sure is that I wanted to join them, where they were. Whatever I had to do to make sure I was able to be with them someday, that is what I would do.

Several days after my session, I received a message from Sid:

I wanted to share this with you. After you left our session a very large black crow sat on the railing of the porch for a few hours. Some of the client's and the owner of the house were a little freaked out but I was OK. I felt his symbolism and thought it was for you. I felt you needed to hear this information since he showed up when you were leaving.

Again, a bird behaving oddly appeared on the scene. I figured it had to be some sort of positive affirmation that communication with the other side had truly taken place. Many traditions consider crows to represent powerful transformations.

Both Sid and Gary indicated to me that Stephanie would contact me directly in the near future. Several days after the reading, a beautiful Monarch butterfly appeared from nowhere in my driveway, and flew over me car. I felt she was near me. Even though I still missed my daughter, these signs all gave me great comfort. I looked forward to more communication from her with great anticipation. I couldn't wait to hear from her again.

Kalila Smith with Stephanie Link

My experience with Sid was profound and life changing. As much as the death of my daughter forever changed me, so did this communication with her. It was a huge step in my healing process.

I listened again to the CD of my reading several days later and realized that the message was for me to evolve (move forward) spiritually. The green feather was not a feather but a quill. He was telling me to write. My writing will help me move forward and heal. The message was really hitting home now.

Chapter Twelve
In Search of God

"For those who believe, no proof is necessary. For those who don't believe, no proof is possible." ~ Stuart Chase

    I found through talking with other parents who had lost children that it is was not uncommon for a person to lose faith after a child has died. I had been a very spiritual person for most of my life, but when my daughter died, I became unsure of what to believe. At first, I blamed God for taking her away from me; then doubted his very existence.

    I wanted to have faith to lean on but did not know where to look for it any longer. I envied the other parents who still had faith despite losing their child. I felt so angry, bitter, and alone. All I knew is that whatever I had believed in before had changed. I had changed. I had to find a different route to what I was seeking.

    It is completely normal at first to feel that God has abandoned us. Those of us who believe in God are usually taught that He hears and answers our prayers and we feel very betrayed when we lose someone we love; especially if it is a sudden, unexpected death or it is a child. We begin to question His love, His compassion, and His will. We even question His existence.

    As the EMT's worked on my child trying to save her, I prayed that God would spare her. They worked on her for a half hour as I paced across my driveway, barely able to breathe. I begged God not to take her. But my prayers were ignored. She was taken with no warning, no preparation, and no clues that she was even suffering from the infection that killed her. I felt that God abandoned me when I needed him the most. I felt betrayed.

When I told my therapist that I was not sure I believed in God, she told me to check out something called the God Spot in our brain. This was probably not the best thing for someone in my state of mind to investigate. Supposedly there was an area in the brain that controlled spiritual, as well as supernatural, experiences. My brain was in no condition to absorb and assimilate this kind of information.

I read half of it and fell deeper into depression. Basically what this told me was that not only had all of my psychic experiences not really happened but any and all spiritual experiences were figments of my imagination as well. As if life wasn't hopeless enough for me at that point, this just made everything feel worse.

"So the old saying 'life is a bitch, then you die' is true?" I wondered.

If this was true then there *really* was nothing beyond this life; there was no point to anything. A friend pointed out to me, "without faith, there is no hope."

The fact of the matter is that some speculation surfaced in the late 1990s suggesting that one portion of the brain was responsible for simulating spiritual experiences. This theory was highly publicized mostly by atheists, who promoted the idea that all spiritual and religious experiences were fabricated by this *God Spot*.

In 2012, researchers at University of Missouri revealed that there are several locations in the brain that are responsible for spiritual experiences, not in that they produce the experience but rather respond to spirituality. This is a very different from what was originally suggested over a decade earlier.

"We have found a neuropsychological basis for spirituality, but it's not isolated to one specific area of the brain," said Brick Johnstone, professor of health psychology in the School of Health Professions. "Spirituality is a much more dynamic concept that uses many parts of the brain. Certain parts of the brain play more predominant roles, but they all work together to facilitate individuals' spiritual experiences."

Afterlife Mysteries Revealed

In the most recent study, Johnstone studied 20 people with traumatic brain injuries affecting the right parietal lobe; the area of the brain situated a few inches above the right ear. He surveyed participants on characteristics of spirituality, such as how close they felt to a higher power and if they felt their lives were part of a divine plan. He found that the participants with more significant injury to their right parietal lobe showed an increased feeling of closeness to a higher power.

"Neuropsychology researchers consistently have shown that impairment on the right side of the brain decreases one's focus on the self," Johnstone said.

He added, "Since our research shows that people with this impairment are more spiritual, this suggests spiritual experiences are associated with a decreased focus on the self. This is consistent with many religious texts that suggest people should concentrate on the well-being of others rather than on themselves."

Johnstone says the right side of the brain is associated with self-orientation, whereas the left side is associated with how individuals relate to others. Although Johnstone studied people with brain injury, previous studies of Buddhist meditators and Franciscan nuns with normal brain function have shown that people can learn to increase their spiritual connections during meditation and prayer. Despite Johnstone's research, it is actually during right brain creative processes that seem to enhance the spiritual experience. Later research suggested that there are several areas in the brain rather than one "spot" that increase spiritual awareness.

I thought back on the many times that I felt a Divine presence intervene in my life. There was one instance in particular that could not be explained. Many years ago, I was driving in North Carolina after bringing Stephanie to camp. I had rented a car to visit a friend who lived nearby. I was driving down the highway at about seventy miles per hour. The radio had lost its transmission so I had adjusted it and looked down at the dashboard for only a moment. When I looked back up, there was a line of stopped cars ahead of me. There had been an accident and some furniture had fallen off of a truck.

My first thought was, "I don't have time to stop."

I looked in the rear view mirror and there was traffic in the left lane beside me. There was nowhere to go. I prepared to crash. But all of a sudden it was as if my mind went blank. I shut my eyes and gripped the wheel tightly. Then out of nowhere, something pulled the wheel to the left, hard. The car glided into the left lane seamlessly and around the pile up. When I opened my eyes, I watched the pile up in the rear view mirror just as the car that had been behind me, hit the one that was stopped in front of me. I would have been sandwiched in between those cars, but something pulled me out of harm's way. To this day, I cannot explain how this happened, other than Divine intervention. Something or someone protected me that day.

Dr. Gary Schwartz, PhD, is a professor of psychology, medicine, neurology, psychiatry, and surgery at the University of Arizona. In his book, *The G.O.D. Experiments*, he used science to prove (or disprove) the existence of an Almighty Creator who reigns over this life and all eternity. Dr. Schwartz uses G.O.D, which stands for guiding, organizing, and designing process to represent whatever his reader's interpretation of God is. He then uses science to prove the existence of a higher power.

Of the many common experiences reported by people who have had NDEs is that these people return with renewed faith in God, in addition to no longer fearing death. The interesting thing it that what they and Dr. Schwartz have in common is the idea that God represents unconditional and infinite love. No matter which stone I turned, at the end of the day, the message was love.

In his documentary, *Afterlife*, director Paul Perry interviews various people who have had NDEs. He also interviewed experts in the field, Dr. Jeffrey Long and Dr. Raymond Moody.

Dr. Long stated in the documentary that over ninety percent of those who experienced NDEs see deceased loved ones during their experience. He also noted that NDEs had massive commonalities, regardless of culture or religious belief. But in each case, the experiencer returns with a firm belief in not only an afterlife but the existence of heaven and a loving God who exists there.

Regardless of the source, most recorded NDEs returned to consciousness with a renewed sense of spirituality, stronger faith in God and an afterlife, no longer fearing death.

Having grown up in a very spiritual environment, losing faith was huge source of discord for me. During my deepest depression when I felt that there was nothing more than this life, no God, no eternal life, I felt empty and hopeless. As my body began to become more balanced and my nervous system became calmer, I was able to rationalize my feelings much better. The truth is I had not stopped believing in God, I had just become so angry that I lost sight of Him.

In researching the NDEs, I realized how many people experienced them, were specifically told that it was not their time to die, and returned. In his book, *Evidence of the Afterlife*, Dr. Long documented that most of the experiencers specifically recall being told by either an actual figure or a disembodied voice that they must return. Some were told that they had specific work to accomplish that was not finished and others were given a choice.

In one case, he wrote of a woman who had been diagnosed with a terminal illness. Her husband was awaiting test results regarding her organ function to determine if her organs were beginning to shut down indicating the early stage of death. During her NDE, this woman is given a choice. She was informed by someone on the other side that if she chose to remain there, her test results would indicate that her organs were indeed shutting down. But if she chose to return to her life, the test results would indicate that she was not shutting down. (Long, 184)

His findings were simply amazing to me and represented a turning point in my grieving process. I had become so angry and bitter that my daughter was *taken* from me that I could not comprehend, nor was I willing to speculate, that perhaps she too might have had a choice. I was unable to think past my own pain. Even though it had been suggested to me shortly after she had passed away, it was not until I read of this woman's experience in Dr. Long's book that it really made sense to me.

A couple of days after my daughter's death, I visited a friend who is also a counselor. He could not see me as a client but agreed that since it was something urgent, he would see me at least once to get me past the initial trauma. His attitude immediately was that although she was no longer in this world, she was somewhere. He suggested that I start to look at different ways to relate to her on this other plane.

He said, "You still have a relationship with her, it is just going to be different now. You have to learn now how to relate to her on these new terms."

He also gave me another perspective to consider. He said, "You did not want her to go. But what would she have wanted? Let's assume that Stephanie had the opportunity to choose to either return to her body, which was in pain and deteriorating from Alzheimer's and she knew what the future held for her in that state, or to cut it short and leave this world. Which one would she choose?"

I had to say, of course, that she would definitely choose to not return to her physical state that she had in this life. He made me look at the fact that I was focusing only on what I had wanted, not what she might have chosen. At the time, I was not ready to accept that this might have been possible. Again, when I read Dr. Long's book, my mind became more open to other possibilities. This shift in thinking became a great comfort for me.

Given the weird circumstances of my daughter's sudden death, no symptoms, no warning, no response to antibiotics, no fever, defying the odds, I had to somehow accept that not only is there a God but He had taken her peacefully in her sleep, sparing her an awful alternative given her diagnosis with early Alzheimer's disease.

Several friends in the medical field had told me early on that given her prognosis, what lie around the corner for her was pain and loss of her cognitive skills. One friend made the comment that her death was a *blessing in disguise*. This hurt me deeply when it was said, but I later realized it was perhaps a blessing for her, just not for me. She died quietly without pain and without fear, instead of a slow deterioration of her mind and body, winding up on feeding tubes in a nursing home. Perhaps my friend was right when she corrected herself and said that it was not just a blessing but a gift. It was I who could not accept it and became angry at the loss. If given the opportunity to decide, I have no doubt my daughter would have not chosen to live that way. I had to accept not only an existence of God, but to accept that He was also merciful. I tried my best to begin to focus on being thankful for what precious time I had with my daughter for almost thirty years. Her life was without a doubt my gift.

Chapter Thirteen
Angels

"Believers, look up - take courage. The angels are nearer than you think." ~ Billy Graham

People who have come back from NDEs, as well as those on their deathbeds, often report seeing deceased loved ones who greet them on the other side. They also report being assisted by angels. But what exactly are angels?

The Catholic Encyclopedia describes an angel as:

...a pure spirit created by God. The Old Testament theology included the belief in angels: the name applied to certain spiritual beings or intelligences of heavenly residence, employed by God as the ministers of His will.

Angels are often used by God to relay messages to humans. Angels can also guide, protect, and heal. They are God's representatives who work with us on our physical plane.

There are many orders of angels. The ones that intercede here with us on the physical planes are the lower orders. They serve as guardians and messengers. They should always be treated with respect, but not worshipped.

The highest order of angels is the Seraphim. They guard God's throne in heaven.

They praise God by saying Holy Holy Holy is the Lord of Hosts. (Isaiah 6:1-7).

These fierce guardians of God each have six wings; one pair cover their feet, another cover their faces, and the other for flying.

The second highest order of angels is the Cherubim. Many people are confused about them, thinking they are chubby little infant-like angels. They are quite the contrary. These angels are large with four faces; a man, an ox, a lion, and an eagle. They have four wings covered with eyes and the body of a lion. Their feet are that of an ox. They, too, praise and protect the Almighty in heaven. The cute, chubby baby-like winged creatures depicted in art are actually called putti and they are secular artistic creations.

The Thrones or Ophanim are found where the material world begins. They are described in the Bible as wheels within wheels with the rims covered in eyes. They are close to the Cherubim.

When they moved, the others moved; when they stopped, the others stopped; and when they rose from the earth, the wheels rose along with them; for the spirit of the living creatures [Cherubim] was in the wheels. (Ezekiel 10:17).

The Dominions regulate the duties of the lower angels and make God's commands known to them. The Virtues control the elements while the Powers protect the cosmos and humans from evil spirits. These powerful warriors are also called Potentates. Together, this second sphere governs the heavens.

The third sphere includes the Principalities, which rule over the material world and Archangels. There are seven main archangels. Michael is actually the prince of the Seraphim. He is often depicted wielding a sword, as it was he who slays demons. He is the leader of God's heavenly army.

Gabriel is seen throughout the bible as a holy messenger. He was responsible for delivering the message to Mary of her immaculate conception. He sits at the left hand of God. Raphael is a healer and is the patron saint of medical workers, matchmakers, and travelers. Uriel is the fourth Archangel and the one who led John the Baptist and his mother, St. Elizabeth, into

Egypt. Selaphiel is the archangel of devoted prayer. Raguel is referred to as the archangel of justice, fairness, harmony, and vengeance. And the seventh is Anael the archangel governing love.

Another lesser mentioned archangel is Metatron, the angel of life. He guards the Tree of Life. In contrast, Ezekial is the archangel of death and transition.

The lowest orders are merely called angels who work on our behalf to help us. These are the messengers and the ones people often describe seeing in their final stages of life and in NDEs. They assist us and comfort us during this transition. They have also been known to comfort loved ones during their grief. Many people believe that these guardians are with us from the time we are born until we cross back over that other realm.

My friend, Gary, was a songwriter who often wrote songs that included angels. He told me one time, "Everybody thinks I make these lyrics up. But it really isn't me," he said as he pointed up, "it's them. They give it to me."

My daughter, Stephanie, talked quite often to spirits. Many believed it was actually angels. I don't know, but one thing was certain, she was never alone. She could be up in the middle of the night and I would hear her talking to someone. Sometimes she would tell whoever it was, "Be quiet, my mom's coming. Quiet."

Whenever I would ask who she was talking to, she would always say, "Oh, nobody."

I would often hear her start talking again as I walked away. She would say, "Okay, she's gone now."

On one occasion, I heard her tell *someone*, "That was a close one."

Several years ago, I left Stephanie with a friend while I made a business trip to Miami to do research for my book, *Miami's Dark Tales*. My friend called me in the middle of the night very alarmed. It was storming in New Orleans and she had gone downstairs to check on Stephanie to make sure she was not frightened from the storm. As she entered the room, she overheard Stephanie talking to someone.

She asked, "Stephanie, who are you talking to?"

Stephanie looked at her with a very serious expression on her face and replied, "The one who makes thunder and lightning."

My friend, a Voodoo priestess, called me immediately telling me that my daughter had conjured Chango (the orisha of thunder) in her living room and she wanted me to have her make him go away. To me, the orisha are no different from angels, as these African spirits are also created by God to intercede in our human affairs and help us. They are all basically the same, but in different traditions, they have different names. At the end of the day, spirits created by God are spirits created by God, no matter what you want to call them.

My friend, Kim, whose daughter has cerebral palsy, recently told me that even though her child cannot speak and is confined to a wheelchair with a feeding tube, when she brings her to church she sees her eyes wander around and her mouth move as if she is seeing and talking to *someone*. She believes that her daughter sees angels in church and holds conversations with them. These special children have their own angels that watch over them and protect them.

In some Jewish sects, children like these are considered extremely special and holy in God's eyes.

The secret is that they remain as they were above. While the body is flawed, the soul inside remains the same as above. The one state resembles the other. Therefore, they are to be renewed like the moon, as it is written (Isaiah 66:23)

They believe that special needs children are highest to God's consciousness and here to teach lessons to others. It is also believed in this faith that God gives us certain *tools* in our lives in order for us to serve our purpose here. For those who were given less *tools,* it is because they did not need them. It is believed that children like my daughter and my friend's daughter are the most elevated and purest of souls. So perhaps they do commune with the angels.

I cannot deny that my daughter did see and speak to beings that were not seen in this physical plane. The spirits she spoke to on a daily basis were not by her definition, ghosts. She was not frightened by them, and they seemed to be her constant companions. She talked to them all the time: sometimes she would laugh at them (or perhaps with them). She was never really alone. Having seen this interaction for almost thirty years, I have to be convinced that when she left this world, she also was not alone. I had always believed that my daughter walked in this world and the other world simultaneously.

In fact, I now question what connection she made with Gary between the time he left this world and when she followed. The weird thing is that they did not know each other in life. This makes for a strange case of karmic connection. Stephanie was connected to his sister for many years, as she was a special education teacher, and director of the camp that Stephanie had attended several times.

Gary and I had lost touch for many years, reconnecting just a few years ago. When he passed away unexpectedly on May 25, 2012, I put a small altar up in my living room with his picture on it. It was close to that time that Stephanie decided that she no longer wished to sleep in her own bedroom. She had decided to camp out in the living room and insisted on sleeping on the sofa bed.

Someone suggested that perhaps he had contacted her and there was some connection between them during that time. Perhaps it was the reason she wanted to stay in the living room. As I mentioned earlier, she had her own little secret world that she shared with spirits and angels. He too had his own world of angels. I have no doubt that he knew that she would be crossing over eight months behind him, and he waited for her. I do not believe that was a coincidence that they both died on the 25th, only eight months apart and on the eve of his birthday. Only they and the angels knew.

There have been documented events throughout time where individuals have witnessed what they believed to be angels appearing in a crisis. One of the most famous cases was what was called *Operation Auca*, in 1956.

The Huaorani tribe was a primitive group of natives that lived deep in the rainforest of Ecuador. Known for their violence, they were also called *Aucas*, a Quechua word that means *savage*. In the early part of that year, five American Evangelical Christian Missionaries ventured deep into the rainforest in an attempt to bring Christianity to the Huaorani. The tribe had been very hostile to oil and rubber workers in an attempt to defend their land. The military had planned an attack on the natives. These missionaries had gone in hopes of solving the problem peacefully.

But the visit was anything but peaceful. By the third day, all five missionaries were speared to death by warriors of the tribe; their bodies thrown into the river. Several days later, a search party with the assistance of a military helicopter came looking for the men.

Thirty-three years later, the widows of several of the men returned with several other missionaries and medical supplies to find out the truth behind the murders, and risk their lives to again try to bring God's message to the rainforest tribe.

What they learned was shocking. The elderly warriors, who had killed the missionaries, told her that as their husbands' lifeless bodies lay on the beach, the natives heard singing in the sky, accompanied by brilliant lights.

In 2000, Matt McCully, the son of one of the missionaries revisited the tribe and was told a similar story by the few remaining aged warriors and the women who were also present during the slayings. Each one of the witnesses claimed to see lights and hear music. Many people, including many of the Huaorani who have since converted to Christianity, believe that it was angels that appeared on that day to greet and take away the spirits of the slain missionaries.

A similar report was made many years later when a former FBI agent recalled seeing angels appear at a 9/11 crash site in Shanksville, PA. In her book, *In the Shadow of a Badge: A Memoir about Flight 93, a Field of Angels, and My Spiritual*

Homecoming, Lilli Leonardi recounted what she saw in the aftermath of the plane crash that happened on 9/11. She arrived at the crash scene shortly after firefighters extinguished the fire caused by the crash. As she left her vehicle, she smells burning wood and fuel along with the smell of death. She saw bright lights.

She said that the light turned into a fog or white mist of some type, and then began swirling into shapes of what she believed to be angels. She claims to have seen hundreds of angels to the left of the field standing in a row. She described them as having wings pointed towards the sky.

Fearing her coworkers might not believe her she said nothing; for two years. But she could not get the memory of what she witnessed out of her mind. She was also haunted by what she found the most disturbing part of the tragedy; there were no bodies, not one found at the crash site.

Lilli wrote her memoirs of the tragedy in an attempt to help her own PTSD. She hoped by sharing what she saw, she might bring comfort to families of those who lost their lives in that crash.

Through my entire life, I have had instance after instance that would support the existence of these heavenly beings. Far too many others have experienced their Divine intervention, or received messages from them, for it not to be true.

Chapter Fourteen
Watchers, Walkers, & Between World

"It was pride that changed angels into devils; it is humility that makes men as angels." ~ Saint Augustine

I have often written about spiritual beings that were never human. Because I have spent so many years working in and around haunted locations, often I referred to the more dangerous of these beings; those who were not highly evolved. Many people seemed to be attracted to these lower vibrational entities, and I felt it necessary to warn people of the dangers of tampering with these spirits. There are many levels of spiritual beings. Just as angels had a hierarchy, so did the entire world of spirits.

People in paranormal circles love to talk about demons. There are so many self-professed *demonologists* out there who claim to be able to remove demons. I have always warned, "If you look for demons, they will find you."

Hollywood movies make demons, possessions, and dark occult activities look cool and chic. In real life, they are anything but. Over the years, I have had countless terrified individuals contact me with problems that have arisen because they played with negative entities. These beings are cursed, and they roam the physical plane with one agenda; to confuse and deceive humans.

Many religious sects believe that all spirit encounters are actually demonic spirits that intentionally try to convince us that they are our loved ones. I do agree that this can, and no doubt does happen, but I do not think all spiritual encounters are demonic in nature. It is because these types of things do happen that the Catholic Church does not condone using Ouija boards, séances, mediums, or any other method of forcing communication. As mentioned in another chapter, the church has since taken a different stance in spirit communication, admitting that it is not only possible, but highly likely. Personally, I think the main issue is that we forcing something unnatural to occur or are we allowing something natural to happen without provocation?

Not only in Catholicism, but other religious paths as well, frown upon forcing communication. You can entice something dark to confuse and betray you if you force this sort of thing. This is why during spiritual misas, prayers are said for protection and also prayers to remove lower vibrational spirits who might deceive to be removed. Great care is taken during these séances to keep communication natural from ascended spirits who are coming from the Divine. During the misa, participants are very quiet and meditate. We wait for spirit to send messages; it is never forced.

Just as angels have different levels, so do the darker spirits. Demons are fallen angels. They were all created by God. Before the fall, Lucifer was one of the most beautiful angels in heaven. Instead of returning God's love, he rebelled against him. Lucifer, and one-third of the angels, were cast out of heaven to have dominion over the physical plane.

The Catechism of the Catholic Church says in paragraph 393:

It is the irrevocable character of their choice, and not a defect in the infinite divine mercy that makes the angels' sin unforgivable.

Lucifer became Satan and the fallen angels became demons. It is believed by the Church that they tempt humankind to alienate man from God.

Satan himself masquerades as an angel of light. It is not surprising, then, if his servants also masquerade as servants of righteousness. Their end will be what their actions deserve (2 Corinthians 11:14-15).

The fallen angels, sometimes referred to as *watchers*, lusted after human females and reproduced with them, creating a race of giants, the Nephilim.

That the sons of God saw the daughters of men that they were fair; and they took wives for themselves, of whom they chose. There were giants in the earth in those days; and also afterward, when the sons of God came in unto the daughters of men, and they bare children to them, the same became mighty men, which were of old, men of renown. (Gen. 6:2-4)

These hybrid humans were destroyed by God in the Great Flood. Because they were half spiritual beings, their souls remained earthbound as evil, discarnate spirits. These spirits can also wreak havoc on humans. The evil spirits can even inhabit humans. In my other books, I mentioned walk-ins, which are evil spirits that literally walk into the body of an innocent human. They often do this when the person is in an altered state, as in under the influence of drugs or alcohol, under anesthesia, or in a comatose state. This is the reason that the Catholic Church does not endorse activity such as astral projection, as it opens up the possibility for an evil spirit to walk-in. It is interesting to really look at the esoteric reasoning behind some of what the rules of the church are. Most of the time, there is valid cause for concern, and the belief is usually pretty universal with other religions as well.
How does one know if they are being misled by an evil spirit? One does not. That is why it is discouraged to seek out spirit contact and conjure spirits. No one can know if what they are calling forth is indeed what it professes to be. During my contact with my friend, I felt pretty confident that it was really him because the messages were always positive and encouraged me to move closer to God. Nothing about it encouraged me to delve deeper on my own into the other side, or remain depressed.

When Stephanie came through Sid Patrick, her message was of love and encouragement, again pushing me to *move forward*. I believe that she meant not only in my grief but in my faith. An evil imposter might encourage me to continue to pay mediums or send me on some sort of spiritual wild goose chase. During my session, I was encouraged to grow spiritually and that my daughter would contact me directly in time. This felt safe and peaceful.

With most NDEs, the experiencer tells of an in-between realm of existence before seeing the light. Most describe this place as a dark void of some kind. It has been reported by many that they are aware of the presence of other spirits, even animals, in this void. It is reported that some are actually moving forward in this void towards the light, while others stay still, remaining in the in-between space. For lack of anything better to call it, I call it *Between World*.

I have always believed that there is some kind of veil or partition that lies between the physical world and the world of spirits. It would also make sense that there is *something* between the two worlds. You do not just abruptly get thrown from this dimension and physical world into something completely different. There is a transition in between. No one who has experienced a NDE has reported being tossed from our world immediately into the next. There are steps.

In various sources, there is a barrier or boundary of some type that exists; separating the two worlds. While everything in *Between World* was at a slower pace, much like our time here, the other side seemed to be at a faster pace. During one of my dream visits with my friend, he once commented to me, "Twenty years on your side is like ten minutes for us her*e*."

This would make sense, given the fact that the energy on that side would be vibrating at a faster rate. Higher vibrational frequencies are found in spiritual beings, especially those higher to God's consciousness. I have often described negative entities as *lower vibrational beings*. A good example of this is when I became attuned as a Reiki, a form of Japanese energy healing. My vibrational rate changed. I was no longer able to wear a watch, as I now depleted the battery. My life force was now at a different rate than what it had been.

In most sources, the NDEs were aware that there was a point in the barrier that once crossed; the person would not be able to return. Some individuals were allowed to make a choice whether to go beyond the barrier; others were specifically told that they were not allowed. When I had my dream of Gary in the house with the fishbowl windows, I was told by my *guide* that I was *not allowed* go inside or tap on the window to get his attention. I was told, "You cannot do that, it is forbidden."

In that particular dream, I was informed by the guide that I should consider myself lucky to be allowed to see that they were okay. I was told that I should not expect, nor ask for, more.

I have mentioned in a previous chapter that my daughter walked in both worlds. I had always felt that my friend, Gary, did as well. They both always seemed rather otherworldly and sometimes even disconnected from this world; he with his music, she with her little secret friends. To many people, I too walk in both worlds, to a certain degree. I always have. In my books, I have often described my experiences throughout my life with spirits. I attributed my connection to spirit to my own NDE as an infant. I have no recollection of the event other than what my mother told me. I was born, then had to be revived, due to respiratory distress of some kind. Stephanie's heartbeat stopped in utero; I heard the monitor. She was taken by emergency C-section and revived. It seems that having NDEs, or even coming close to death, opens up something in the psyche that makes one more susceptible to walking on both sides and spirit communication. It is for this reason I became so frustrated when I was not getting more communication from my daughter from the other side. I expected more because of my experiences throughout my life.

In the foreword of *The Afterlife of Billy Fingers: How My Bad-Boy Brother Proved to Me There's Life After Death* by Annie Kagan**,** Dr. Raymond Moody discusses what Greek philosophers of ancient times called *walkers between the worlds.*

These walkers were living people who could move between the two worlds and acted as messengers from the other side. Today we call them mediums, and they serve the same purpose. According to what Dr. Moody describes, Stephanie was one such individual.

In Shamanism, the practitioner goes into an altered state to contact spirits on the other side for messages and healing. The Native American tribes, and other early tribal cultures, usually had spiritual leaders that served the same purpose in the community. These great healers often received messages from spirit in dreams.

In a dream state, we can move freely in Between World, which is why so often see spirits of our loved ones, as well as our guardian spirits can communicate with us, when we are dreaming. In my most recent spirit dream, I was in a beautiful field, and have vivid memories of that very real place. I know that I could not possibly have been in heaven, but where I visited was very, very real. It was too vivid not to be. It had to be somewhere in Between World. It was not just an ordinary dream.

Chapter Fifteen
Visions of Heaven But What About Hell?

"Death and love are the two wings that bear the good man to Heaven." ~ Michelangelo

After I made contact with Stephanie through Sid Patrick, I was flooded with questions that I should have thought of while he was communicating with her. I wondered about where she was. I felt very relieved to know that she was not alone. Finally, I believed that she was in a *better* place, but what was Heaven like?

According to most NDEs, there is a Heaven; a beautiful place where we spend our eternity. It is Paradise. It is the home of God, Jesus, the Saints, and all of the Angels. It is a place that those who have visited the other side and returned call *home*.

The Catholic Encyclopedia describes Heaven as such, "There is a Heaven, i.e., God will bestow happiness and the richest gifts on all those who depart this life free from original sin and personal mortal sin, and who are, consequently, in the state of justice and friendship with God."

In the dream that I had the night of Sid's reading, when I met with Gary in a field, it was extremely vivid. Greens were greener, blues were bluer, clouds were big and fluffy above, and the cool breeze blowing my hair gently across my face smelled of fragrant flowers. Everything about that special little meeting place in my dream was very vibrant; picture perfect. Certainly, if this place in my dreams was so beautiful and perfect, the real Heaven had to be even more so.

Kalila Smith with Stephanie Link

Dr. Moody not only studied thousands of NDEs in his life, but had his own NDE. He feels that when we leave the physical body, we merely go to another state of consciousness. He described this other level as completely different from what we experience in this plane of existence. He stated in the documentary, *Afterlife* that our language on this plane is unable to accurately describe what the other level looks like. Many theorize that Heaven is really another dimension. Whatever it is, those who return that have seen it are forever changed by what they experience. Many people, including the mediums that I've met, believe that Heaven or the afterlife is a particular place, so much so that is a parallel dimension.

It is common belief that we possibly create our own heaven. If this theory is correct, then Stephanie's version would be paints of all colors, bright and vivid. It would be filled with colored butterflies. Rainbows would gently fall across white fluffy clouds. As I wrote this, these images popped into my head. I think of what Sid Patrick told me when he said that these things are coming from *her*. It was as if she was showing me what she saw on the other side. I continued to write as my mind slipped into Between World. I no longer needed to read what NDEr's had seen. I saw vivid pictures in my mind of where Stephanie was now. I quieted my mind and allowed the pictures to become a movie in my mind's eye. It was as if I had remote viewing capabilities to see the scenes that she was showing me.

As I wrote, I allowed my mind to relax and tune into to her messages. I saw brown and white ponies, much like the ones she rode as a small child, prancing through meadows of soft grass blowing in a gentle breeze. I saw Jasmine and Baby Dog running in the field, as Stephanie walked alongside them in a white flowing dress, amongst dazzling yellow flowers. She was surrounded by butterflies. She smiled happily. This scene is somewhat like some sort of lucid dreaming. It was as if my ability for visualization just amped up a few notches. I could smell the flowers and the sweet grass!

I closed my eyes again, relaxing my entire body. I took a deep breath. There is a clear water of some type running alongside of this scene. More like a stream than a river, and there are large rocks beneath very shallow, rapidly moving water. We have nothing like this in South Louisiana. All of our water is dark and murky, so this is not a memory. The water is cold. I believe this is Stephanie, describing her surroundings to me as I write. I consulted with Sid Patrick and he suggested the same thing. That she was showing me where she was.

The scene is very similar to the one where I saw Gary in my dream the night after Sid made contact. Is this the Between World where can meet and make contact? I had to let the process flow where it needed to go.

My concentration broke, I began to analyze the situation and all sense of communication stopped. Something was definitely happening. I was not sure what though. I continued with my original thoughts.

No doubt whether Heaven was an actual location or a parallel dimension; it is paradise. I finally believed it. Some people believe that there are multitudes of parallel worlds. Medium, Sid Patrick believes heaven is:

...a place of all knowing. I believe when the spirit leaves our physical body that we then go to what I like to call God's court. Here, we review our lives, and are sent to learn our purpose. While there, we are available to assist our loved ones in the physical life if they will listen. Always remember that free will plays a large role in our journey. God will determine the vibration that we will someday return to a physical body to complete our cycle until we reach the heavenly vibration in which then we will not need to return to the physical.

The majority of NDEs that I had researched were all very positive experiences, and the experiencer sees what he/she believes to be Heaven, but does everyone really go to Heaven? Throughout time, there have been very evil people who have committed heinous crimes against others, what about them? Do they go to Heaven too? Surely, not everyone goes to Heaven. It would not seem right if really evil people, like Adolph Hitler for example, went to Heaven just as everyone else. Those who were religious called the ones who claimed all went some place good, false prophets. They believe it is the work of the devil to deceive and encourage people away from God. Certainly there were NDEs that were frightening or hellish.

On February 8, 2013, David Sessions wrote an article for *The Daily Beast*. He wrote:

In March 1992, Matthew Botsford walked out of a restaurant in Atlanta and found himself in the middle of a gun battle. He was struck in the back of the head with a 9mm bullet. Before he knew it, he had died and gone to Hell.

I felt a hot, needlelike pierce, excruciatingly painful, for a brief moment on the top of my head," Botsford wrote in A Day in Hell, an account of what he experienced in the underworld during the 27-day coma that followed the shooting. "Utter darkness enveloped me as if thick, black ink had been poured over my eyes." He later described being "hung over an abyss" as heat blasted up from below. Pairs of demonic eyes crept toward him before a divine entity grabbed him by the waist and said, "It's not your time."

Sessions recounted the 2005 experience of art professor Howard Storm, who wrote about it in his book, *My Descent into Death*.

. . . Howard Storm rose to fame after claiming he had been "viciously attacked" by evil creatures in Hell while unconscious before emergency surgery, an experience he described in his book. He tried to pray, which only provoked the angry creatures. "They screamed at me, 'There is no God!' ... They spoke in the most obscene language, worse than any blasphemy said on earth.

We have little documentation on the validity of there being an actual place of punishment for the wicked. But given the heinous crimes that are committed by people in our world, it would certainly seem warranted for such a place to exist. I cannot fathom evil wrongdoers getting a simple life review and a slap on the wrist then joining the other souls in paradise. It would certainly seem reasonable that we would have to be held accountable for causing pain and loss to others. If what these few sources have documented, it certainly sounds as if hell is very real, and not a place that most of us would want to wind up. Having grown up Catholic I was taught that not only was there a Heaven and a Hell, but also a Purgatory. As a child, it seemed that Purgatory was somewhat of an almost Hell; like Hell but not as bad and you can get out. But more recently, I find that the Church actually considers it a place where souls aren't quite pure enough for Heaven. Purgatory is actually based on the Latin word "purgare" which means to make clean or to purify.

It is a place of temporal punishment for those who, departing this life in God's grace, are not entirely free from venial faults, or have not fully paid the satisfaction due to their transgressions.

It could very well be a place or condition where the soul is purified and has to reflect on the lessons learned in life. This school of thought falls in line with numerous spiritual paths. Some souls may need time to adjust or reflect when they leave this existence. All that has been proven is that *most* people report a beautiful place with a Creator that is pure, unconditional love. If there is a hell, it is some place I would prefer to avoid. Even though I have never had a NDE myself, the experiences that I have had since my daughter's death have instilled in me a desire to become more spiritually aware and evolved. We still do not know if the visions of what people perceived as hellish depicted the "real hell," or if there was some other explanation for it. What is known is that of those who have seen it, they return to this world terrified, and the effects of their vision are life changing.

Chapter Sixteen
Messages Continue

"Of all the haunting moments of motherhood, few rank with hearing your own words come out of your daughter's mouth." ~ Victoria Secunda

One morning as I jaunted off to work, I was greeted immediately by a dragonfly that landed on my chest, right over my heart, and stayed a second or two then disappeared. I laughed out loud but it was not my laugh. It was hers. It just came out of my mouth. I could not believe it. I laughed out loud and it sounded exactly like her laugh. Even though it came from me, it shocked me, as it was completely unconscious. This sign, I knew well had, been sent by Stephanie. From that point on, I felt her presence near me. She always walked in both worlds and just as promised in Sid's reading, she was definitely still halfway in this world. Prior to that, I had blocked what she was sending.

As I channeled Stephanie and saw the movies she played in my mind, I continually changed chapter titles in this book. I began to type just as I had done the automatic writing in early therapy homework. It was no longer my mind choosing what to write, but my hands typing what she described. When I wrote *Searching for Spirits,* I felt Gary's presence behind it, but this was different. She was in my head! Then I remembered something my stepson, Justin, had told me shortly after she died. Justin suffered from bi-polar disorder and schizophrenia, which was controlled by medications. He was deeply saddened to lose his only sister.

Several days after her death, he said he was seeing her in *his head* when he tried to sleep. He told me that he even told her,

"Get out of my head, Steph; I have enough problems as it is. I can't take you being in my head too."

I literally went from one extreme, believing nothing, to the other, believing that my daughter was channeling through me. One would think that this would certainly make me feel as if I was going crazy, but it didn't. On the contrary, I felt very certain that some kind of a connection had been made with her on the other side. This was neither solicited nor forced by my will. I believe that this was originating on her end. She said through Sid that once I was ready, she would communicate more with me. I felt more at peace than I had since her death. She spoke to me through this mental imaging. She showed me her new world.

Unlike the dream where I was in *that place* speaking to Gary, this was more from an objective perspective. In NLP (neuro-linguistic programming), when someone visualizes himself from a subjective perspective, he is associated with his surroundings. The person is in the vision, seeing everything around him through his own eyes. The person is there. Disassociation would indicate the person sees himself from an objective perspective, from outside the body; much like an out of body experience, only it is visualization in one's mind. I was viewing her in that place, but I was not there. It was very similar to the fishbowl house dream, except I was not asleep.

It had been over fifteen years since my days of experimenting with various forms of alternative psychotherapy, but given what I had going on, I figured maybe it was time to revisit some of those modalities to better center and focus myself. A little self-discovery was in order. I signed up to attend a dream workshop the following month.

I had already been going to yoga sessions, which helped with meditation. I needed to give my nervous system breaks from the constant stress and trauma that I had been going through. During meditation, the internal dialogue is turned off. This is not something one learns overnight. I had studied this for many years, but it had been a very long time since I had applied the principles to my life. I needed to reconnect with what I had learned many years before, in order to heal my body, mind, and spirit.

I began my game plan for self-discovery, as I continued to interview experts, attend workshops, and delve into Between World via mediums, automatic writing, dreams, and visualization meditations. I mentioned earlier that a counselor friend urged me to immediately begin to relate to Stephanie in a new way and to explore what those ways might be. When she first died, I put up an altar to her in her room, but I had not tended to it. I cleaned her room, made an altar, and closed it off. I shut it off from the rest of the house and from me. It was just too painful to go in there. This would have to change.

As I drove across the bridge that day to the city, wondering about Stephanie and if she had been communicating with me and if she really was helping write this book, when out of the corner of my eye, I saw a portion of a rainbow on a big, white, fluffy cloud. The sky was crystal clear and the clouds all white and fluffy, not a rain cloud in sight. I've seen many a rainbow coming over the lake, but usually, it is conditions conducive for rainbows. It might have just rained, the sun was just coming out, and a full rainbow would expand over the horizon. This was different. It was a portion of a rainbow, with only three colors, pink, yellow, and green. It was on maybe one-fourth of the cloud, but it was very noticeable. I was driving down I-10 on a bridge, but I managed to put my phone on camera mode and take several photos of it. Afterwards, I turned the camera off and immediately, the rainbow faded into the cloud. I took that as a sign, letting me know that she is with me as I write this, and she my co-author.

Once I was opened to receiving messages from Stephanie, they came more frequently. They came in the form of signs, such as the daily visits from butterflies to messages through other people. Sometimes when spirits come through via a third person, messages are not always obvious or cut and dry. Shortly after her death, my friends Phillip and Avo paid me a visit to help comfort me. Phillip had worked with me as a psychic/medium on numerous investigations and was a very clear conduit for spirits.

Sometimes when someone is too close personally, they cannot pick up anything. I figured it was a possibility, but I certainly was not expecting anything to happen. I was glad to have the company.

Nothing came through to Phillip during our visit. But right before he left for the evening, he walked over to Stephanie's little altar that I had made for her. He stood there for a few moments, meditating, I thought anyway.

Then he asked a very strange question.

He asked, "Where is Fraggle Rock?"

No one else knew what that meant, but I did. I immediately stood up and said, "I'll get it."

I went back to Stephanie's room and retrieved a gift boxed set of television shows from her childhood, HBO's Fraggle Rock. I brought the box out and set it on the altar. Then I cried and hugged Phillip. I could not thank him enough. He had no idea what it meant, but I knew that Stephanie had to have to put those thoughts in his head; otherwise he would have never come up with that information.

One very odd form of communication took place when a friend referred a television show my way. The producer of the show insisted that I make my own video audition for submission. This was only a couple of months after my daughter's death, and the last thing I felt like doing was a video of me. I made every excuse I could not to do this video, but the producer was adamant.

Finally, I reluctantly pulled a small camcorder from my camera bag, one I had not used in over a year. The battery had been so drained it took a day to charge the camcorder. Finally, I managed to muster up enough energy to do the little half minute interview. I hooked the camcorder to the computer to download the footage and to my surprise, there was footage on the camcorder that I had forgotten about; precious footage from the summer of 2011 with my daughter and grandchildren on vacation in Florida.

I never heard from that producer again. It did not matter. The spirit used him and my friend as a vehicle to get me to hook that camcorder up to the computer to see the footage. I have no doubt that the spirit who did that was my daughter. She wanted me to pull that footage and watch it. It was priceless!

One never knows when or how a spirit will make contact. After my friend Angela lost her father, she called out to him asking for him to give her a sign. Her daughter, who was small at the time, would comfort her by telling her, "Don't worry, he's picking flowers with Jesus."

Her father was hardly a religious man, so she worried about his soul. She missed him terribly and wanted desperately to know that he was okay. She sought out a reading with a local medium. The medium picked up on the fact that Angela had brought balloons to her father's gravesite. She also said several other things to her which, while comforting, were a bit vague. Like many people in deep grief, she needed something more to really convince her that contact had been made.

Then the medium informed her, "Your father said 'don't worry, he's picking flowers with Jesus.'"

Angela was shocked, amazed, and relieved all at the same time. She knew immediately that contact had truly come through from her father. She had repeat visits with the same medium, never again having the profound experience she did the first time. She reminded me that the communication I had through Sid Patrick was what she called *a gift from God*. It is not every day to have such communication, so when we do get it, we have to treasure it.

As I waited for the next step on my journey with other mediums, I treasured the messages I had gotten so far. I did receive other signs, although very subtle. One evening, as I came home from work, I noticed that the recliner chair was in a reclining position, and I had not left it that way. I know the cat could not have done it. The recliner was one of those old ones that had a manual handle that had to be pulled to get it to recline. The remote control to the television had also been shoved down between the cushion seat and side of the chair. I had not had any visitors and had not watched TV in weeks. There is no physical explanation for it. Many people would say it was an ADC (after death communication). Until another reasonable explanation comes along, I am inclined to agree.

Chapter Seventeen
The Doctor, The Evidence, and the Verdict

"Death ... Is no more than passing from one room into another. But there's a difference for me, you know. Because in that other room, I shall be able to see." ~ Helen Keller

Dr. Jeffrey Long is a radiation oncologist in Houma, Louisiana. Houma is a small bayou town in South Louisiana, located about an hour outside of my home. Dr. Long agreed to meet with me to discuss his opinions of the afterlife. It was an honor and a pleasure to have an opportunity to meet with one of the great medical doctors who had stepped forward and validated the afterlife with years of research.

As I have written many times, the question of life existing after this physical plane has intrigued and mystified mankind, since the dawn of time. Early pioneers of the Spiritualist movements were considered in their time to be nothing more than over-zealous fanatics and frauds. Even as late as the 1970s and 1980s, NDEs and ADCs were considered by many to be nothing more than wishful thinking of the faithful or New Age fluff.

As a student of alternative therapies, much of what I studied many years ago was considered edgy or occult. Today, a lot of the same once alternative therapies such as hypnotherapy are considered quite mainstream now. Dr. Raymond Moody wrote *Life After Life* in 1975. This was not considered to be true science at that time. A near-death-experience, a phrase he first used in that book, was met with much of the same skepticism by scientists and medical doctors as table tipping of the Victorian era. Professionals in the world of science gave little to no validation of the phenomena. Dr. Moody and Dr. Kubler-Ross, both psychiatrists, were the pioneers in these studies. They were met with great controversy during the early days as well. Their experiments and documentation were considered metaphysical in nature rather than true science.

I can remember in the 1970s as a teenager when I had a fascination with spirit communication and afterlife questions. I had seen/heard unexplained phenomena my entire life. By the time I was in my teens, I began to question these mysteries. At an early age, I believed that there had to be an explanation for what I had been experiencing my entire life. It was also at this time that I became aware of my intense fear of death. During my teenage years, three young people died that were relatively close to my inner circle. There had also been instances where others close to my age, but not necessarily in my social circle, had died. This disturbed me. That horrible feeling one gets when someone you know dies unexpectedly can be extremely disturbing. The person is there one minute; alive, animated, and you have even spoken to them, then suddenly, without warning, they are gone-forever.

In my early life, I questioned, "Where did they go?"

I asked this question again at age eighteen when my father died. I asked again two years later when I lost my mother. By the time I had suffered my third miscarriage, I stopped asking. It was this uncomfortable feeling of indescribable loss that drove me to delve into paranormal investigations later in life. Throughout the early 1980s, there was little information available on the subject. I did not begin to investigate paranormal activity until the mid-1990s.

It was not until many years later when more data was obtained and more medical doctors began to delve into the mysteries of the afterlife. Dr. Jeffrey Long is one of those doctors who began to question what happened to us after death.

I contacted Dr. Long after watching the documentary, *Afterlife*, and noticing that it was filmed partially in the French Quarter. He was kind enough to meet with me and discuss his feelings on the afterlife. We met for lunch in the quaint little town of Houma, in southernmost Louisiana. Driving from my home in Laplace to Houma is a mere hour jaunt through the swamps and bayous of South Louisiana. You know you are in the swamp when the only road kill you see is the occasional alligator on the side of the road. In Houma, the bayou is literally up to the side of the road. It can be a bit unnerving, even if you grew up down here. Houma is one of the South's hidden jewels.

Upon meeting Dr. Long, I expressed to him my gratitude because I wondered if he realized what a great contribution he had made to people like me, grieving the loss of a loved one. I expressed to him that someone like me clings desperately to the hope that there is an afterlife and that I might one day reunite with my beloved child in that other existence. The validation that he and others like him bring to the existence of an afterlife is priceless to the grieving. It is this evidence that gives us comfort and hope. The more we know that our loved ones are enjoying an afterlife, the more we can move past our pain and keep our loving memories alive. Having experienced the loss of a child, I have come to realize that proof of an afterlife is the single most important thing in healing grief. Those who are grieving a death of someone we love know that we can never have the life that we once knew with that person. The next best attainable goal is to know unequivocally that our loved one still exists, and is somewhere safe and comfortable. We need to know that they are no longer in pain, and that they are with others who love them. It is the only way for some of us to survive the loss and discover ways to grow through the grief process.

I felt honored that he took the time to meet with me and discuss his thoughts. Knowledge of the life hereafter humbles us. There is no pretentiousness, no inflated egos, nor arrogance. Those who have proven these facts and know what lies ahead have no need for frivolous attitudes. Like the ones who have experienced the NDEs and come back to tell of it, life changing views replace old attitudes. Dr. Long was one of the most affable, gracious persons I have ever met; very down to earth. It was very comfortable to be in his presence.

The first thing he said to me was that he believed without any doubts that there was most definitely an afterlife. He went on to say that those who are there are absolutely in a better place than we are in this life. If reading his book and others that affirmed that there is a life after this one was not enough for me, to see this man who had spent years of his life documenting NDEs, thousands of them, look me in the eye and make those statements drove it all home for me. I felt a sense of peace come over me like a blanket covering my soul. It is almost indescribable what I felt at that very moment, to hear those words from him.

In his book *Evidence of the Afterlife,* he outlined evidence proving that life exists beyond this physical existence. Dr. Long documented thousands of NDEs over many years. Some of the most remarkable NDEs are those that he conducted with people who were blind since birth. His point of course is that these people return with NDEs describing scenes that would be impossible for someone with no reference point of sight. People who are born blind cannot describe seeing something they have never seen in life. Yet, these people have the exact same experience and see the same things that people with perfect vision have.

Dr. Long stated, "There is one thing my research leaves me very clear on is that there absolutely is an afterlife. We absolutely go on, all of us; and the afterlife is wonderful! These are the kind of things that I spent most of my life taking on faith. The majority of other people who believe in life after death have done the same. But as you know from reading my book, I think the evidence is *so* strong and I've had a lot of consideration about that. I've literally spent hours deciding if the evidence was strong enough and I'd be ready to say to the world that at least in my opinion, that there is evidence of life after death. The answer is obviously yes. I am very, very cautious about making such statements. For me to come out and say that the evidence is that strong; for me to make that announcement to the world that there is life after death, is a big deal. It just took me a while to get there. I needed to be sure and ultimately, well, you read the book, I'm sure."

I asked Dr. Long, "I've noticed that most researchers of NDEs report that the experiencers tell about very positive experiences. They see a beautiful place and a loving God but what about negative NDEs? Does anyone ever come back and report having a negative experience? Were there any hellish NDEs?"

He responded, "The scholarly term for that kind of experience would be 'frightening or distressing' NDEs. The reason is because even with the most distressing or frightening experiences that I've ever heard in my life of these near death experiences, they've had positive outcomes from it. In other words, it is very common that when they have these experiences, they will learn from them and understand that there was no other way that they could be reached. They realize that they had very serious issues that had to be confronted so that they can be better people."

This, of course, brought up for me the issue of some individuals believing that NDEs are demonic or the work of the devil. This is a common belief among many Christian sects. But I believe that the evidence overwhelmingly proves that even when an individual has had what might be perceived by some as a demonic or hellish NDE, they return even more so with a renewed belief in God and the existence of an afterlife. The argument for many people who believe that these experiences are deceptive maneuvers that are really Satanic in nature is that the devil is the great imposter and loves to trick man into moving away from God. If this were indeed the case, then these people who have NDEs would certainly not be moving closer to God. So it is absurd to even suggest, in my opinion, that the experiences are anything other than real and these people are being exposed to the other side and experiencing God's work first hand.

In my own spiritual path, I've been told that if we do not listen to what spirit is telling us, where spirit is directing us, sometimes spirit or God will stop us in our tracks to get our attention or teach us the lesson. For some, it is not as extreme as actually experiencing a NDE. I have certainly firsthand knowledge of people who had been struck with illness or an accident that hindered them temporarily, forcing them to make certain changes in their lives. Many people have made life changing decisions after a debilitating accident or illness. For others, a NDE is what puts them back on track spiritually. And still for others, it might even be the death of someone close to them. I have heard more than one medium state that their turning point was losing a beloved family member. Without a doubt, losing my daughter was a life changing event in my life. Everything in my life changed in that one moment when she left this world. I will never be who I was again. When faced with these life changing and spiritually awakening moments, we have to make a choice if what we experienced is going to serve us for the better or worse. In the case with NDEs, that decision seems to always be for the better.

Dr. Long went on:

So, even when these experiences have been distressing or frightening, they have the potential for being enormously life changing. So that's why they're called distressing or frightening rather than negative. There's no question. The problem in working with frightening NDE's, even the hellish ones, the difficulty is what is frightening to one person is not necessarily frightening to another.

There was one instance where the person was in an ambulance, being taken to the hospital, and had an out of body experience over the top of the ambulance. During which time angels had come in and surrounded the person. Most people would say 'Oh, that's so wonderful.'

Well, guess what? This particular person was quite frightened and was batting at the angels. So it's a subjective experience. I think the best research approach in studying frightening experiences is to study those that have content that is objectively frightening.

A very significant number of NDEs that were considered hellish were often people who had been in bad accidents and suffered substantial injuries. But a lot of times when they awaken from what they perceive as a hellish NDE, in actuality, they awaken to find that they had been in a coma for two weeks, and they may have experienced ICU psychosis.

Dr. Long continued, explaining that sometimes after traumatic accidents, particularly when the individual has an out-of-body-experience and sees their own body injured below, this can be so extremely distressing then they wind up in ICU in a coma, continuing to focus on what they have seen and experienced. It is not a true NDE if their experience was what is called 'ICU psychosis,' which is a hallucinatory experience that may happen with a prolonged ICU stay.

He explained, "NDEs can occur while in a coma, but it may be difficult to be sure the experience was a NDE and not ICU psychosis."

Dr. Long has strict criteria for documenting experiences on his web site to discourage false claims and attention seekers. When asked if some people fabricate their experiences for attention, he responded:

Not everyone who represents that they had a bonafide spiritual experience really did. My study requires that those reported NDEs must fill out a questionnaire with a hundred-sixty questions. So they are usually pretty sure that they've experienced something real to invest that kind of time. The postings are anonymous so there is no recognition for the sharing the experiences. It cut downs on attention seekers. Nobody is paid to share their experience on our NDERF website.

I then asked him, "Where does karma and reincarnation fit into this scenario?"

He responded:

Kalila Smith with Stephanie Link

In the U.S, twenty-percent of the population believes in reincarnation because the United States is primarily Christian. On the other hand if you go to other countries, Buddhists in particular, the great majority of the people, 80 percent or more, believe it's a reality. I think it's obvious to anybody who is familiar with NDEs that there is pretty strong evidence that there is reincarnation. And I would suggest that reincarnation is possible. We could not believe that the universe is infinite if something, like reincarnation, is not possible. To say something is not possible in an infinite universe is a contradiction.

One of the things that help validate the NDE and the existence of past lives is that virtually all past lives that are described in NDEs are very mundane. Many people who want to believe in reincarnation would like to believe that they were someone famous. Just as an example, a lot of people have this romanticized version of the medieval city. One person who had a NDE and a past life remembrance in a medieval city said the streets were muddy and narrow and it stunk. This is how medieval cities typically really were. It had a lot of poverty, a lot of derelicts; it was a highly undesirable place by our current standards of city life. So that was a real medieval city. You can't get that from watching Disney. I have a questionnaire that alludes to the question: do you believe you had an existence prior to your earthly existence?

It's almost impossible to word that question accurately, to give responses related only to prior life remembrances. Reponses to this question as written will give some information about whether they had a spiritual, unearthly existence or if they had an actual earthly life prior to this life. Some people do describe a prior life in a physical realm that is not earth, but this is very uncommon.

We have had a number of past lives where they were very aware of whom they were in this other life. They had the same personality as this life. The evidence is strong that there is a potential for past lives.

The personality traits they have in this life may have existed in their described prior earthly life. You don't usually see karma described in their experience. It doesn't mean that the karma isn't operating. It just means that they are not aware of it.

I don't believe the classic karma, in the sense that if you step on a spider; you come back in a later life as a spider.

The one thing that is very common and is overwhelming in NDEs is that they are aware of overwhelming love and overwhelming knowledge. There is overwhelming acceptance, and we are a part of it; we often just don't know it. So really as far as having a "debt" to pay from our earthly life mistakes, I don't really see that in the NDE. I think that we are certainly responsible and accountable for what we do here, but I think we are all part of a big picture. One thing we can do in the afterlife is plead ignorance. Perhaps we can laughingly try to explain our earthly shortcomings in the afterlife by saying, 'look how dumb we were in this life!'

It becomes more of a learning thing than anything. There seems to be a real connection between everyone and everything.

Dr. Long confirms what most other experts do; there is an afterlife. Life continues after the physical death on this plane of existence.

Of his many documented cases of NDE, a large percentage of these specifically contain a point during the NDE where the experiencer is told that they must return; it is not their time. In certain cases, some were actually given a choice to either continue across the border of no return or to go back to their earthly incarnations. This was extremely comforting to me. It reinforced that there is a Divine plan in this universe and we all have a purpose. And when our purpose is fulfilled, we return *home* to a loving and compassionate Creator.

If God uses anybody on this earth as a vehicle for His work it is people like Dr. Long. Not only has this man made his life's work trying to save lives and heal those suffering from cancer, but the many years he has spent researching and documenting proof that there really is an afterlife, is truly God's work and necessary for those who grieve for their lost loved ones.

Chapter Eighteen
The Afterlife Awareness Conference 2013

"There is an afterlife. I am convinced of this." ~ Paulo Coelho

During the early days of my intense search for answers, I stumbled across a website, Eternea.org. At first, the name created images of some futuristic fantasy site. It is actually a site where science meets spirituality. Its mission is *to support and engage in scientific research, public education and practical programmatic initiatives to further awareness and acceptance of the fact that eternal existence in some form or manner is a fundamental reality for all living things as an inherent quality of nature.* Near death experiencer and medical expert Dr. Eben Alexander, along with Dr. Jeffrey Long, were among the many medical professionals affiliated with the organization. It was on this site that I found a link to the Original Afterlife Awareness Conference that was meeting in June 2013 in St. Louis. My sister-in-law, Patti Jo, invited me to attend with her as my birthday present.

As I prepared for the trip, I happened to receive a note in the mail one morning. It was from the mother of one of Stephanie's friends. I had shared with her the dream when Stephanie had given me her phone number. When we spoke at my daughter's wake, she mentioned to me that Stephanie had called Troy a few weeks before she died. Troy was not home when the call came in and his sister wrote a message down, "Stephanie called for Troy."

Apparently, his mother had kept the message for Troy. She indicated that she believed that Troy was getting visits or messages from Stephanie. She wrote that he kept bringing the message to her and showing it to her saying, "my friend."

I tried, but failed, to contact her before my trip. I hoped to talk in more detail about what she might be experiencing. Stephanie seemed to be making the rounds with friends. Her former caretaker, Crystal, is a technician at our veterinarian's office. When I brought my animals in for their visit, she informed me that Stephanie had been appearing in her dreams regularly. In fact, she told me that aside from Stephanie, the only other person she had ever gotten messages from was her grandmother. I was happy to find that as I prepared to seek further contact with my daughter, others were getting signs and messages from her, as well. I left for St. Louis with great expectations.

On the drive to St. Louis, Patti Jo and I discussed the many people who had died in our family, with my daughter and brother being the most prominent. One of the people we missed dearly was an aunt who was Japanese. Her name was *Fujia*, but we all called her Aunt Kay. Patti Jo shared a story about Aunt Kay that happened shortly after her death many years ago. Aunt Kay had been working on origami for Patti Jo, a type of Japanese artwork. She died before the piece was finished.

Several weeks after her death, she received a call from a friend of Aunt Kay. The Japanese woman could barely speak English, but relayed to her that she had seen *Fujia* in a dream and that she had been instructed by her to complete the artwork. My sister-in-law informed her that she had no idea where the origami was in her aunt's house. The woman replied in her broken English, "That okay, she told me where is."

The woman contacted Aunt Kay's husband and asked if she could get something from the home. He agreed. When she arrived, she knew from her dream exactly where to find the origami, and was able to complete the project for my sister-in-law.

*****

Afterlife Mysteries Revealed

We arrived to in St. Louis the evening before the event began. This was an event like no other. The conference is the brainchild of Terri Daniel. Terri is a grief counselor, a hospice worker, a death transitional therapist, and an author. Much like me, Terri was propelled into pursuing the afterlife after the death of her special needs son, Danny. Like my daughter, Danny began to communicate with his mother from the other side. Terri wrote several books while communicating with Danny. The bond between a mother and child is very strong. This is particularly true when the child is special needs. These children are sent to this world with very specific lessons to teach those of us who are fortunate enough to have them in our lives. In two separate medium sessions, Stephanie had confirmed that she choose me to be her mother. The lessons we learn from these children forge a bond that can never be broken. I now know that we remain connected to these kids after they have crossed over. Their ability to communicate back and forth between worlds seems to be easier for them.

In an interview with Edge Magazine online, Terri stated, "This conference is an extraordinary opportunity to look at death and bereavement in a new light. Our audience is made up of hospice workers, scientists, therapists, clergy, spiritual seekers, the bereaved and the curious. We've all found, throughout our years of practice, that understanding how consciousness continues after the death of the body is a key to providing wisdom and comfort for the bereaved and overcoming the fear of death.

On my first day, I spent the morning in a grief workshop with spiritual bereavement facilitator, Christine Duminiak. Christine began working with the afterlife in 1998 after a surprise visit from her in-laws. What made the visit different was that they were both deceased.

She discussed the most common types of ADCs and the effect of them on the grieving. Without a doubt, from my own experiences, I was very much aware of how these signs and communications from the other side were able to heal grief and give hope of being reunited with loved ones in the afterlife.

ADCs are meant to bring comfort. Sid Patrick had discussed during his reading that spirits cannot hurt or bring pain. There are imposter spirits who deceive by impersonating loved ones, bringing confusion and intensifying grief. Our true loved ones, who reside with God, know no pain or sadness. They bring comfort and reassurance and their visits are often during dream states. They are no longer suffering and they do not want us to suffer.

Most people who work frequently with ADCs believe that as long as one is aligned with God, keeping themselves grounded; it is safe to communicate with the other side. When I asked Sid Patrick how he avoids dealing with deceptive spirits, he responded that he always prays and asks for God's protection.

Receiving a dream is not something we are provoking. These signs and messages come to us sometimes when we least expect it. Most of the time, we are not trying to force something unnatural to occur. When a medium opens up for communication, they merely are open. They are not forcing anything, either. Most mediums will tell their subjects that they cannot predict, force, or guarantee communication.

In her book *Embracing Death*, Terri Daniel wrote about negative entities, "If you have a frightening experience in meditation or channeling, simply state, out loud, 'I would like to understand and work with this energy to move it toward the Light." (100)

Other signs can be experienced as touches, sounds, chills, a weight on the bed, a feeling of peace, their scent, or ears closing up. I found this interesting, as I had many instances since my daughter had left when I felt a strange sensation in my ears, as if they were heavy or closed up. I thought it was an allergic reaction or sinus problem. More signs included the typical electronic devices being changed or turned on/off, butterflies, dragonflies, birds, or other animals behaving oddly, and telepathic thoughts forming in our minds.

Christine discussed ADCs that manifest through communication devices; telephones, answering machines, caller ID's, and similar manifestations. I had read the same thing on various websites for ADCs. I have to admit I was very skeptical about these types, having never received one of them.

Apparently, however, my daughter must have been present during this workshop because during the weekend, I experienced two very weird telecommunication ADCs.

The first happened on Saturday evening, the night after the grief workshop. I had just recently upgraded my cell phone to a new phone and synced my Face Book account to my phone. I was sitting in a medium demonstration by Suzanne Northrop. My phone alerted me that I had a photograph in a social network page in which someone had tagged me. I clicked over to see who sent it and it was from Stephanie's account. It was a photo of her from Halloween. She was dressed in a vampire costume with blood dripping from the corners of her mouth. It was sent not once but twice. No one has access to her account or information; only I did. The following day, I had an inbox message on my social page again from her account. There was no message attached, just a notice that she sent a message from her account. It was as if she was testing the system to see if she could really communicate that way. It was very surprising.

Another way that our loved ones attempt to show us love and bring joy and comfort to us is a gift from nowhere. In my case, it was in the form of a beautiful red flower that grew in the back of my neglected back yard. There was no garden. Nothing had been planted there, yet a single red flower grew and bloomed along the fence. Unfortunately, the gardener hacked it down while cutting the lawn. It was not before I managed to capture a photo of it. I know it bloomed for me, and that my daughter sent it as a gift.

This workshop also reminded everyone to refrain from questioning ADCs. This is how I drove myself crazy in the beginning. Part of grief is feeling as if everything is unreal and we begin to question the gifts we receive. Grief is what stops the connection. Those on the other side cannot connect to us when we are consumed with negative emotions. Unless we are centered and balanced, we cannot properly receive and comprehend the messages from the other side. This is difficult in the beginning, but many ADCs occur in the three-day period following a death and, especially in the case of children. Therefore, it is important to attempt to maintain your balance and pay attention to what is being communicated.

Christine's workshop was topped off with a guided meditation opening us up to visitations from our loved ones. During the meditation, I felt my daughter sitting next to me, on the arm of the chair. I felt her arm around my waist and her head on my shoulder. She was there!

One point she made was that some souls have a more difficult time on the other side than others. Some souls, like Stephanie, quietly slipped over and found themselves in God's presence, enjoying His love and acceptance. Others have trouble forgiving, and allowing them to be joined with God. Some remain separate, unable to communicate with us. These souls need our prayers and love to help them evolve and grow closer to God. This is a common belief in many religions. In Catholicism, as well as Voodoo or Santeria, we pray for souls of the dead that they may elevate to God.

The grief workshop reminded all of us that ADCs are gifts from God. They are gifts of love from those that we love on the other side. She stressed that sometimes we have to request that our love ones contact us. She also encouraged us to show gratitude for the contact that we receive and acknowledge them as gifts. She also advised not to analyze the contact; just claim it and be thankful. People who receive ADCs are definitely more peaceful and comforted than those who do not. In my own grief journey, ADCs are what helped me to work through my loss. Knowing that my daughter is still with me is what keeps me going. I can still feel my daughter's energy all around me.

In *A Swan in Heaven*, Terri Daniel wrote this about her connection to her son, "At the same time, even in the midst of unbearable grief, I don't actually *miss* Danny. This probably sounds heartless, because for most people dealing with a death, the greatest pain is in the glaring absence of the person they were so close to. To me, he is not absent at all. He's closer to me now than he was in physical life, and this proves over and over again that we humans exist on many levels beyond the physical, and that love is a life force which vibrates through us all as a connecting fiber, regardless of whether or not we have bodies. Love truly never dies" (136).

The next day I had hoped to attend a workshop conducted by Dr. Eben Alexander on his NDE documented in his book, *Proof of Heaven*. This workshop was one of the highlights for me, and one of the main reasons I attended the conference, like the Gestalt cliché, life happens when you are planning other things. Life had other plans for me. Every time I said or thought anything about the workshop, a thought entered my mind, "No, you want to go to the out-of-body-experience workshop."

I never considered doing the OBE workshop. It is not something I had ever considered trying. But it seemed that my daughter, who had made it very clear that she was in attendance, wanted me at that workshop instead of Dr. Alexander's. Trusting the messages she sent to me, I diverted myself to the OBE workshop Saturday morning.

I was somewhat familiar with OBE, but had always avoided attempting them out of fear. I learned many years ago that sometimes people do not return to their bodies or can open themselves up to walk-ins; discarnate spirits wanting to remain on the physical plane or evil spirits looking for a host. The attitude about OBEs had changed since the 1980s.

William Buhlman had been experiencing and teaching OBEs for twenty years. He uses the technique to explore the different dimensions, and to enhance his life here on the physical plane. Although having never really explored this option, the class was a new concept for me. It would take more than a two-hour class to wrap my head around this practice, and probably a lot longer to actually try it out. However, I felt Stephanie sitting on the arm of the chair leaning against me. She whispered in my ear, "This is how I did it."

Finally, it made sense to me. She was trying to show me how she had walked between worlds all the time she was on this plane. Because she was so spiritually evolved, even though she was handicapped by our standards, she came into this life quite adept at leaving her body and traveling between worlds. I instinctively knew that she wanted to share this with me. She also wanted me to explore the possibilities and give it a try. I told her I was open to the possibility, but it would take some time and studying before I would feel comfortable enough to try it. I could feel how excited she was to share this with me. It was a very special as well as a very different kind of mother/daughter experience for us. The most important part of the conference was yet to come for me. I scheduled a session with an artist medium to see if she would draw a sketch of Stephanie.

Chapter Nineteen
Photographic Evidence

"A picture is worth a thousand words." ~ Napoleon Bonaparte

The morning after my daughter died, when I caught a glimpse of her sitting on the edge of my bed, I saw for the first time what my child would have looked like had she not been born with Down Syndrome. She was beautiful! Even though I always thought my daughter was beautiful no matter what, I was in awe at how beautiful she was without the physical disabilities associated with DS. She had silky, thick, dark hair that shined in the morning light. She had the very distinct nose that she had in this life. Her face was not as round though. Her eyes were much larger. She looked very much like a blue eyed version of her older sister.

From the moment I saw her like that, I wanted to find an artist who could replicate what she looked like in a sketch or painting. I was not sure how to go about finding that. As I write this, my printer is turning on and off again on its own. This tells me that Stephanie agrees with this quest.

Janette Kay is an artist medium who draws the spirits who communicate through her. Oddly enough she does not see the spirits she draws. Much like with automatic writing, she channels the spirit and her hand draws their image. She conducted a demonstration of her unique gift along with medium Dr. Paul Coleman at the conference. I decided to see Janette for a private session in hopes of capturing Stephanie's image in a drawing.

Janette immediately felt the presence of what she described as a younger female. She felt several people who wanted to make contact with me, but I told her that there was one in particular that I was hoping to get. She asked, "The first impression I'm getting; did you lose someone who was younger than you who looked similar to you?"

I answered, "Yes."

She said, "I get the feeling she is saying that she looks somewhat like you; like you had a similar face."

"Yes, she looks a lot like me," I told her.

Janette asked, "Alright, so let me see. The next one that's happening, I feel like I'm seeing sidewalk chalk. And she likes crayons, things like that. I don't know if I'm being taking back in time with the person, or if it's present time. But to me I'm seeing like little kid's toys. Does that make sense with this person?"

I responded, "Yes."

Janette asked the next question, "Did she pass when she was younger?"

"Yes, she was younger than I," I answered.

She then said, "But that's what I don't always know but for whatever reason she's taking me back to that little kid time."

Of course I did not want to as they call it, *feed the medium*. Mediums generally tell their clients not to give them information but rather allow the person on the other side to give them details. The information she was getting of course related to Stephanie since she had DS and was very much like a younger child throughout her entire life.

Janette went on, "The other thing that's happening. She is making me see something in here."

She ran her hand across her upper chest. Of course I related immediately because Stephanie died from pneumonia. So again, this made sense. I acknowledged but did not elaborate.

"To me it feels like it was an ongoing health situation, if that makes sense," she said.

I agreed. She then said that she saw little hearts around the girl indicating that she had a lot of love for me. This was extremely comforting to me.

"It feels so pure and sweet. It has a little girl quality. She is giving me a number six. Six, sixteen, something like that," she said.

Janette saw the date on the wall like a calendar. That did not make sense to me immediately but later on I did realize that it was my confirmation that my brother was also present. He died on June 6, 2008. Janette suggested it was a birth or passing of someone else.

"I feel like she is showing me that you visited her in a hospital," she said.

I confirmed.

"She is trying to comfort you. That is what it feels like to me. She shows you walking through the door. She wants to let you know that she is okay. It feels like she was trying to comfort you. She doesn't want to see you be sad. She is showing me wiping tears away. She is telling me, 'Don't cry, Mommy,' She wants to acknowledge that but it's just a couple of seconds then she's joyful again. She is such a joyful spirit. It's almost like you can't take it out of her. It's like negative after negative, this then that and the other thing, but she's just dances right by, like she couldn't be beat," she said.

"That's Stephanie," I said.

Janette then told me, "I feel like she was one of these spirits who came here to help other people learn some things. I don't normally get into these things on readings but she makes me feel like she chose you to be her mother. She's like 'of course, I picked her.' I don't know if you believe in shared lives connections but that's why she's bringing it up. But it feels to me like you have been together before and you will be together again."

Janette continued, "I feel like she wants to show me something. She is showing me inside her mouth."

Again, this made perfect sense because she had just had her tonsils removed when she died. Stephanie went on to show

Janette that she liked her hair in pigtails. I used to put her hair up in pigtails when she was little. This was in line with what she said to Sid Patrick about liking her hair brushed and styled.

Stephanie also told Janette that her father was miles away but she still looked out for him. This message was very significant. There is no way that Janette could have possibly made up any of the information but especially to know that her father was "faraway" and that she still cared for him nonetheless. She always loved him although she had not seen him since she was a baby. This was a tremendous confirmation for me.

"She's makes me feel very bright and inquisitive. I feel like she liked school. Does that make sense? She is saying she didn't have a very long life but she says she had a really good life. She couldn't find anything to complain about. She is showing me toys, a mom that was so good to her; so no complaints. She had a really happy life. So, you know I feel like she talks about it being hard and difficult for you. She shows me you with books and movies and she's a part of that," Janette said.

"I'm actually writing a book, and she's helping write it," I told her.

Janette continued, "It's almost like you see the world a little different and she's a part of that."

Janette began to draw my daughter's face. As soon as she drew the eyebrows, I could see it was her. When she was done, I saw on the paper the same girl that I saw sitting on the edge of my bed the morning after she died. It was Stephanie without the physical features of Down syndrome just as I had hoped.

While Janette was drawing her, Stephanie told her about the signs she had sent to me and how in tune we are to each other. She also mentioned the horses she used to ride in her life. She also told Janette how much she loved art and loved to draw.

The following day, Patti Jo also did a session with Janette and wound up with a drawing of my brother. She drew him as he looked when he had lost his hair because of chemotherapy. During the last days of his life, my sister-in-law shaved him leaving a mustache on him. He never wore a mustache but she gave him one just to be funny. He chose to appear in the drawing like that to show her that it was really him. The mustache was a personal joke between the two of them. The rest of us didn't even remember him ever having a mustache until she mentioned the incident. It gave her a tremendous amount of comfort after five years of being so grief stricken and cut-off that she didn't see any of the signs. After she returned home, now that she was open, her ADC's increased as well.

Chapter Twenty
Death Bed Experiences

"Somebody should tell us, right at the start of our lives that we are dying. Then we might live life to the limit, every minute of every day. Do it! I say. Whatever you want to do, do it now! There are only so many tomorrows." ~ Pope Paul VI

The deathbed experience is another form of compelling evidence that life exists after death. Many people have visions of spirit beings or deceased family members that are seen just before they die.

In *One Last Hug Before I Go*, author and psychotherapist, Carla Wills-Brandon wrote, "Since I've been collecting accounts of DBEs, family members have often asked me about another deathbed phenomenon known as the 'Stare." (92)

She referred to *the transfixed gaze* that many people have shortly before they die, usually focused on the ceiling or foot of the bed. Many medical professionals wrote it off in the past as just how someone looks when they are dying, but today, it is recognized as how someone looks when they see either angels or recognize deceased loved ones waiting for them. (Wills-Brandon, 93)

When my daughter died, a friend who is a registered nurse, Kathryn, spent the night at my home. She shared her stepmother's deathbed experience in hopes of giving me some comfort. She remembered her mother experiencing the *stare*.

Grace suffered from bladder cancer. She had spent a great deal of her illness on dialysis. When it became apparent that her quality of life was not going to improve, Grace decided to end her treatments and check herself into a hospice facility. She had spent the past year and a half in medical treatments. She had grown weary and was ready to move on.

For over a year, she was on a strict diet, due to her dialysis. She had to limit her sodium intake so she could not enjoy a lot of the foods that she once had before she became ill. Before checking herself into the facility, the family had a party for her. She drank beer and ate pretzels. She enjoyed crackers with cheese and salami. She ate her favorite foods that she missed, and reminisced with her children and other family members. Then she packed her things and checked herself into the facility. The staff was surprised that she walked in rather than allowing herself to be wheeled in a wheelchair. Although her children were sad that she was leaving them, they respected her wishes and made her "party" as festive as possible.

Kathryn accompanied Grace to the facility to check her in. Her room was filled with her favorite flowers, long stemmed yellow roses. Grace loved birds and had always enjoyed sitting on her patio watching and listening to them. She had a sound machine with the music of birds playing in her room. During the night, all of the roses had opened up, filling the room with their fragrance. Her room smelled and sounded like a beautiful garden. After checking in, Kathryn went to work calling periodically to check on her.

Eventually, Kathryn was informed by a sibling that Grace was *breathing funny*. Kathryn, being a nurse, was familiar with Cheyne–Stokes respiration. She explained, "You breathe kind of fast then you stop breathing for a short amount of time, and basically it's the first sign of dying, that the organs are shutting down. It's not long after that, that you're actually gone."

Knowing she was limited on time, Kathryn hurried over to the facility to sit with Grace in her final hours. Kathryn sat at her side holding her hand. A step-sister sat on the other side of her, reading the Bible, and her step-brother sat at the foot of the bed. Grace had been given pain medication and something to help her relax so she was not alert. Her family consoled her with loving messages; letting her know that it was okay to go. Grace continued to breathe sporadically, but suddenly, turned her head and opened her eyes. She fixed her gaze at the corner of the ceiling and smiled wide at "something." Then she closed her eyes for a moment, and looked and smiled again at another corner of the room. She then took her last breath.

Kathryn said, "My oldest step-brother (Grace's son) died several months before. We really feel that he came for her. It was pretty amazing. It was one of the most phenomenal things I had ever experienced."

Kathryn spent many years as a hospice nurse. She described her step-mother's death as one of the "most peaceful, beautiful deaths" she had ever seen.

Another friend who is also a nurse, Angela, shared her mother's deathbed experience with me. Her father died several years before. When her mother had become weak and in her last days of life, she announced to Angela that she had been visited by Angela's father. Angela, not knowing how to respond, allowed her to give her account of it. Much to her surprise, her mother told her, "You know what that means don't you?"

Angela asked, "What does it mean, Mom?"

Her mother answered, "Well, your father is dead, and it means that I'm going to die soon, too."

Back when I first dated my ex-husband, his mother was dying of cancer. I had sat with her a couple times to give him a break. At one point, a few days before she died, she told me that she had been visited by her "deceased husband."

She was completely aware that he had visited her and was dead. She did not indicate that she knew what it meant, but she was in hospice and had chosen to stop treatments, so certainly she knew she would be crossing over very soon.

Kathryn said that she had really only seen one death that was what she would describe as difficult. A man clung to life, struggling his last few hours, not wanting to pass on. He literally fought to breathe all the way to the end, when his body finally gave out. She mentioned that Grace should have lived another couple of weeks, but was so "ready" to move on that she died in a couple of days, instead. This brought up an interesting point. There had been cases where clearly people either waited to see a family member before they died or waited until someone had left the room to die without them present. Why were some people given the opportunity to choose? This was a question that would take further investigation if it can be answered at all. Certainly people who suffered sudden death were not given such a choice.

Not too long before my daughter died, a friend of Kathryn's was killed suddenly in a motorcycle accident. She had just heard from him in a text message and within a few moments, he drove his motorcycle onto the interstate, and was hit by a truck. He died instantly. Nothing is more shocking than to speak someone one minute and know that they are dead the next. She told me of another time in her life when she had just seen someone and then they were killed in an accident. Only in this case, she wondered if on some level, the person knew that they were going to die.

Many years ago, she attended a social function with friends. One of her male friends gave her a ride home that evening. On their way home, he began to tell her what she perceived to be very strange things. He told her that he wanted particular friends to know that he liked them. She felt somewhat uncomfortable with the conversation, and kept insisting that *he* should tell his other friends how much he appreciated them, but he kept insisting that she make sure they know how he felt. There was a young woman he was particularly fond of, and he even instructed Kathryn to tell her of his fondness. She thought his request was a bit odd. Of course at the time, she had no way of knowing what would happen later that night. She just thought it was an odd conversation, and left him that evening feeling that something was somewhat *off.*

The following morning, Kathryn received a call from a mutual friend, informing her that the man was killed that night in an automobile accident. It was almost as if he knew that he would never have the opportunity to tell his friends what he felt. I had heard of similar stories from others.

A couple of years ago, I was called in to do a paranormal investigation in a club called Cadillac's. I knew the owner, and he was having problems with his employees complaining that the place was haunted. They had reported seeing the apparition of a

Afterlife Mysteries Revealed

young man in various parts of the building. As it turned out, twenty years earlier, the keyboard player in a band had been killed there. As he left the side entrance of the building to put his gear in his car, he was struck by a drunk driver who had left moments earlier. She had gone through the front doors and wound up driving on the wrong side of the highway. She quickly turned onto the side driveway to avoid oncoming traffic, just as he walked through the side door. She struck him as he exited the club, killing him instantly.

That band was scheduled to play at the club for their thirty year anniversary and last performance. I felt certain that the keyboard player was merely making an appearance to be with his buddies one last time. This would be an anniversary for him too.

When I interviewed a band member who was his best friend, he informed me that on the night that the keyboard player was killed, he told his best friend how much he loved him and had a look on his face as if he "would never see him again."

There are countless similar stories over time that have cropped up making it seem that on some level, some people do know when there time is up. There is no way for us to know for sure. It is another one of the unexplained mysteries of death we cannot understand. Sometimes there are other clues when someone is soon to die.

Many years ago, I knew a medium named Mitzi who could tell when someone was going to die by how their aura appeared. An aura is a body of light that emits from our physical body. Some people are able to see colors within. We are made of much more than our physical bodies. We have an energetic body that surrounds us. This can be felt very subtly by trained energy healers. Our life force radiates beyond our physical body and can be seen. Kirlian is a certain type of photography that captures the electrical charges that is emitted from our bodies; our life force. Mitzi could see changes in auras that indicated someone was going to die soon. She called it "seeing someone's light bulb go out."

Shortly after my daughter's death, a very close family friend began her own journey to the other side. During her life she was very close to my daughter. "Betty" was seventy-eight when she was diagnosed with terminal cancer. Patti Jo and I were attending the afterlife conference when we received a call from Betty's daughter, who informed us that the doctor had told the family that she might not make it through the weekend. That call came in at the end of the conference. The final event for the weekend was a closing ritual, which included what appeared to be a Shamanic ritual. The last thing was some sacred Hawaiian music. Betty was from Hawaii. When I told her daughter about the music, it gave her some comfort. Perhaps Stephanie had something to do with the choice of music that afternoon.

After I hung up, I heard Stephanie's voice in my mind telling me, "Tell them to play Hawaiian music for her."

I had to call back to relay the message to her daughter.

Shortly before Betty died, my sister-in-law noticed that her aura had changed colors. Most of us cannot see others' auras, but Patti Jo has always had the ability without really trying. When I was a teenager, it was a novelty to bring friends over to her house so she could tell us what color auras we all had.

In between workshops and lectures at the conference, she had some fun in the bookstore at the aura photography table. She told people waiting in line for photographs what their auras looked like and what it meant, then to everyone's amazement, the photo would show the color that she had seen. She never was really into working on psychic abilities and in her early life, assumed that everyone saw colors around people. But at Betty's deathbed, she was shocked to see her aura had become very small and close to her body, turning a dark purple. Violet or purple in auras usually relates to the crown chakra at the top of the head. Interestingly, it is at that point that many have seen a white mist leaving the body at the time of death.

Patti Jo was disturbed to see the change in the aura. She had never noticed that kind of a change in anyone else, so it startled her to see what was once a large glowing blue and pink ray of light had now compressed and darkened. I assured her that it was probably normal, and indicated that Betty would soon be leaving this world. But the aura changes prove that death occurs on many different levels in the both the physical and astral body.

When we last visited Betty, she was barely conscious. Her family attended to her, making her as comfortable as possible. She died peacefully a few days after our visit. Once again, someone close to me died, but not while I was present. I wondered if perhaps Stephanie was there to welcome her to her new world. They had been so close for so many years and Betty died five months and a day after my daughter. It would not be appropriate to bother her family with questions about what she might have seen or experienced. At some point, if something did happen that anyone noticed, they would let me know.

Betty crossed over several days after a super moon. On the night of the full moon, as she lie unconscious in her bed, her son took some photos of the moon. When we later looked at them, he saw the image of his mother reflected in the clouds above the moon. Her facial features and hair were very prominent. Across her neck was a Hawaiian lei. Everyone who saw the photos agreed that it was her.

One of the highlights of the conference was a lecture by the father of NDEs, Dr. Raymond Moody. His most recent research expands beyond NDE and deathbed experiences. He found that often times, in addition to the person dying experiencing visions from angels and deceased loved ones, bystanders (family members and medical staff) experience what the dying person does simultaneously. They sometimes see the other spirit beings manifesting during a visitation but more recent documentation tells of these bystanders actually experiencing something similar to NDE. There have been actual cases where someone present at the time of death escorts the dying person to the tunnel up to a certain point in Between World. Some have even reported sharing the experience of a life review with the dying.

Dr. Moody pointed out that these experiences prove beyond all doubt that "there is some other kind of existence other than this."

The living person who shares the experience is not deprived of oxygen nor heavily medicated. They are not in a coma, nor in any altered state of consciousness. Yet they have vivid recall of what they see, hear, and feel during the death of another person. This is a fascinating discovery. Third person validation proves that deathbed visions are real. NDEs are real. This defies all so-called scientific explanation. We now know that third party individuals can telepathically connect in Between World and escort the dying to the world beyond this one.

As I sat listening to him speak, I could feel my daughter next me. I knew that she wanted me to attend this conference. I could feel the happiness she felt that I had done as she asked and was moving forward. The more I experienced and learned, the closer I could be with her on the other side.

When I returned home, my friend Bobbi shared her experience when her father died, many years before. Even though she was not present when her father died, she had some sort of OBE that created a bilocation. She was in two different places at the same time.

It was January 11, 1986. All day long, she had felt the urge to contact her father. She kept putting it off, involving herself in other things, but in the late afternoon her mother called and told her that she was not feeling well. Bobbi got caught up in her own activities completely ignoring the urges to contact her father.

She explained what happened that night, "Later that night when my husband and I were getting ready for bed, we relaxed for a while, watching television. Suddenly, the house phone rang. As my husband talked on the phone, I had this strange, out of body experience. It was as if I was physically in two places at the same time.

I could hear him talking, but at the same time, I had this vision of my dad at the foot of my bed. He just kept saying over and over again, 'I'm so sorry, I love you.' Standing behind him, I could see my grandmother (his mom who had died five years earlier) and with her was *her* mother, my great grandma Carrie. I never met Carrie. She died three months before I was born. I had only seen pictures of her, which is how I recognized her.

During this vision, the two kept telling my dad that it was time to go. I don't know how long it was, seconds or minutes, but it was so real. I could touch him; touch them.

Then I came back to the room and heard my husband tell someone on the phone, 'I'll tell her.' Then he told the person on the phone, 'We'll be right over.'

When he hung up the phone, he informed me that my dad was gone. He had died earlier that day. He said I screamed a shrill high pitched scream, but I don't remember it. Everything from that point on was a blur in my mind.

Bobbi later learned from her mother that during the same time that she had her bilocation vision, her mother, in a different location, felt chest pains in her body simultaneously.

Although what she experienced was not exactly what Dr. Moody discussed, it still represents the unexplainable phenomena that can occur at the time of someone's death. What we do know is that people do reach out to loved ones. The dying receives a welcoming from the ones who have passed before them. Those they are leaving receive good-byes sometimes. There is no rhyme or reason to the sequence of events that take place. All we do know is that it is love that connects us to others on either side.

There is a bond that cannot be broken, even by physical death. There is so much more to learn and explore about communication and visits during the death process and beyond. We have only hit the tip of the iceberg in discovering how and why some people experience what they do. It does continue to give credence to an afterlife existing. Physical death is only the end to the life that we knew on this level existence. Something else inside of us, our souls, spirits, whatever you want to call it, lives on. Love continues. We can communicate and reach one another on both sides.

Chapter Twenty-One
How the Mediums Work

"Being a medium who can communicate with souls isn't the same as one who can interact with them. It's the difference between listening in on a conversation and changing the subject."
~ S. Kelley Harrell

I had an opportunity to delve a bit into the minds of the mediums to see just how they are processing their information. What they do is very similar to what Phillip and I have done on paranormal investigations. The biggest difference is that their messages are a bit more self-contained and directed to specific people, whereas what we do on investigations can be much more generalized and specific only to the location, rather than a particular person. They not only have to assimilate and interpret the message, but figure out who it is directed to.

At the Afterlife Awareness conference, there were forms available for those who wanted to volunteer, so I filled one out and had the opportunity to "audition" by introducing one of their featured mediums, Ara Parisien. I wound up being the person who gets to run around the audience with the microphone for participants to talk with the medium. I had seen it done before, having attended demonstrations by John Edwards and Suzanne Northrop. It's a lot different than how it appears when you are merely seated and observing. I got quite the workout that night.

Ara Parisien is a natural born psychic medium and Transformation Coach, who has been offering personal and group reading sessions and coaching to people across the globe for over twenty years. She is clairvoyant, clairaudient and clairsentient, which provide her clients with a diverse field in which to learn, grow, and empower themselves. Ara has also worked on numerous missing persons cases.

Her book, *The Other Side of Grief*, tells of how her work as a medium can help in working through our grief. Because she walks in both worlds and knows that life continues after physical death, she views loss and grief from a totally different perspective.

She wrote, "Grieving is a process we will all experience to one degree or another. I do not believe it is a process that realizes any successful completion; rather it is a journey through anguish to something more bearable and then on to something more manageable. The journey is an evolution in and of itself. It is a journey into the past and the future that eventually leads us back to the now" (113).

She describes mediumship as a "dance" between the medium and the deceased. She wrote, "The art of mediumship is like a grand dance. Mediums raise their vibrational rate as high as possible while spirits lower theirs and meet the medium halfway. Then the dance ensues" (79).

After being "microphone girl" for a gallery session, I'd call it more of a marathon. As mentioned earlier, things on the other side move at higher vibrational rate and everything is faster there. We are vibrating lower and slower. When I receive messages from my daughter, entire thoughts are zipping into my mind at very high speed, faster than I can mentally assimilate them. I've noticed sometimes I wind up forgetting what popped into my mind because it is so high speed. It works well when I am writing because I type faster than I can process a thought. I can literally type and not think at the same time.

Melena Landry is a medium from Lafayette, Louisiana who is on the board of the Afterlife Awareness Conference. She also works with Sid Patrick in New Orleans at his Metaphysical and Healing Center. She has seen and heard spirits since she was a child.

She told me, "I had been bugged by the spirit world to do the work but had always refused. I had an experience with a friend who was dying. His spirit would not leave me alone until I gave in. I was very stubborn. I argued and set all these ground rules in place, thinking I had won. Well, with no advertising, which was one of my ground rules, I read one person whose mother would not leave me alone. I called the woman's daughter, a friend of mine, and explained that we needed to meet and why. I wound up talking to her for three hours. When I returned home a voice told me, "You see. This is why you need to be doing this work. This is why we have your back. Look at how many people you can help." I told my spirits to bring the people and I will do it, but I won't call anyone again and tell them that their family is bugging me. Well now, people find me. I stay booked three and four months in advance at all times."

Melena shared a story about the first time she realized that she had a connection to the spirit world in her early childhood:

The first time I ever remember arguing with a spirit and having them actually talk to me was when I was about five or six years old. I was walking back from my great grandmother's house. The wind blew in my face. I remember a very peaceful feeling coming over me and hearing a voice say to me, "It's a great day for someone to die today." I remember answering back, skipping back towards my grandmothers, and saying "Yes it's a wonderful day to die." Then I stopped and thought how could you think that? Then I heard the voice again. I remember telling myself to stop thinking that and how awful that was to wish or even think that someone would die.

Then I thought about people crying and the darkness of the funeral home and how bad I felt for thinking this. When I got home, everyone was acting very different. I wondered if they somehow knew I had those awful thoughts in my head. I believed that they were angry with me. A little while later, my grandmother told me that my hamster died. I remember them being very surprised that I did not cry or become hysterical, as they might expect. I did, however, secretly blame myself. I believed that I caused my pet to die because of what had popped into my mind. When in fact, much later, I realized that I did not cause the death of my hamster. I was given information about the pet dying from a spirit.

    Melena knows what lies on the other side. She says it is beautiful, filled with joy, peace, and love. Although she cannot describe in words things that she has seen there, she knows that it is our true home. It is where we originate, not merely where we end. She believes that most of the spirits she communicates with are merely moving between realms. She says that some do remain more earthbound to stay close to loved ones, but most watch from a distance and allow those they love to live their own lives without interference.

    She did acknowledge that some spirits do get stuck or can be confused, especially if there was a sudden death or something traumatic. This makes sense to me as a therapist. When we suffer trauma or unexpected, sudden loss we are in shock and denial for some time because of it. It is completely reasonable to think that some spirits might also suffer from the same on the other side. This might account for what we traditionally call an intelligent haunting. I have done investigations where the spirit was not aware of what had happened. This would also account for spirits that have been described in NDEs as those in the tunnel who did not move forward. Prayer can help these spirits complete their journey. Melena prays to angels to come and assist these lost souls to completion.

*****

    A group of friends gathered on a Sunday evening in late June for a gallery style reading from Sid Patrick. This is similar to what I saw at the conference, but instead of over one hundred people, there were only nine of us. I was so pleased with the reading I had gotten from him, I recommended him to others, some of whom preferred to share a session rather than do private ones. I brought my sister-in-law, who found the Afterlife Awareness Conference and her session with Janette Kay to be so healing and life changing in her grief process, which she wanted to explore further opportunities to hear from my brother.

When she met with Janette, she mentioned that she feared her grief was holding my brother back. She did not want to prevent his spirit from evolving. He responded by saying besides looking after her, he wasn't doing anything but fishing. Perhaps he'd have more to say tonight. I hoped so. I welcomed more communication from Stephanie as well.

We were joined with my friends Kim and Angela and several of Kim's friends. Everyone was hopeful. I had attended recent gallery sessions with John Edward and those who were featured at the conference, Suzanne Northrop and Ara Parisien. I did not have anything come through for me in the group sessions; only in private sessions. Generally in a group setting, the more people attending, the less opportunity there is of something coming through for "you." It seemed in large groups, what came through was often for people who were together in small groups.

Regardless who the medium is, that person cannot control what or who comes through. It's basically luck of the draw, unless you are in a private session. Even then, there is never a guarantee that the person who comes through is going to be who you want to hear from. The medium has no control. Spirits do not perform on demand. This is why during large group sessions; the medium is running back and forth in the audience. Spirits pull that person in all directions, depending on who is coming through for whom. Most mediums agree that messages come through as needed. Those who need the messages the most will get them.

Sid Patrick explained:

The spirit world uses what the medium knows to reach out to them. For example, I am a nurse, so they use my knowledge of medicine to show me things. The spirit knows how to reach the medium and we all differ. Another example might be one medium might see a clown to get the feeling the spirit might have been funny in their lifetime. However, my sign for funny is the hat that

Kalila Smith with Stephanie Link

Minnie Pearl wore with the price tag. The spirit is highly intelligent and knows how to communicate with the medium. A good medium will sit with spirits daily to develop a relationship. I have a way to signal them when it is time for me to work. Only occasionally they will visit if needed, but mostly they respect my wishes. My sign for them is when I take off my wedding rings and begin my introduction.

The gallery reading with Sid was pretty low-key, as galleries go. Many of the people who attended had never experienced a medium before. I did hear from my mother, which seemed weird. I had not heard anything from her in so many years. But it was nice to find out that she was proud of me. My brother also came through with another message for my sister-in-law, urging her to live her life. That was a real comfort, since she was still so shut down after five years. She had purchased several books at the conference, so hopefully between the books and the messages; she would be able to feel more at peace. Stephanie did not come through, but I pretty much knew that she would not. I had received so many recent messages from her, and I was now getting messages from her directly, so it was no surprise. Several others received messages from their deceased family members, as well.

After the reading, Sid shared some photographs from some of his travels with us. He also discussed with the group his studies to pursue physical mediumship. The readings that he currently conducts are very similar to the others I had seen recently. They are what are called mental mediumship. The medium sees/hears/feels, usually in his/her mind's eye, various symbols or messages and translates them to the clients. Physical mediumship is different.

Sid explained, "The mental medium connects with spirit and receives messages through one of the body's senses, such as clairvoyance, which is clear seeing. Physical mediumship is when the medium produces physical phenomena, such as table tipping, direct voice, trumpet and other object movement, creation of ectoplasm and any other type of physical evidence."

I asked Sid how he knew that what was coming through was really the spirits of deceased loved ones and not something deceiving. He responded:

A spirit that communicates is a God sent spirit. This is a spirit that has been through God's court and is on a high vibrational plane. A haunting can be one of a couple of things. Sometimes it is a negative energy that has not left the plane. Example would be if a murder happened in a home, which energy can linger. A sensitive may come into the house and experience some strange events or even take that energy with them. A spirit that is on a low vibration can also create some paranormal events. As a medium, we stay connected to God's higher vibrational spirits and do not allow the negative to interfere in the work we do. Some spirits are stuck because they choose not to leave or may not realize that they should cross over. Mediums many times will assist with that crossing over.

I have been called to investigate several negative incidents. Usually they are related to a specific incident or person. I have done many house cleansings and have assisted with ridding two people of negative energies. These were not particularly disturbing to me, but the people involved were scared. These energies can really challenge someone's belief system and this is usually the first step in recovery. I try to understand the client's belief system and work from there in assisting them back to a baseline. I practice in the light of our Lord God and never give energy to the negative. Most mediums will protect themselves and their beliefs. I have never encountered a lower vibrational being while working with spirits during a medium's demonstration.

My sister-in-law called me two days later to say that she realized that her aunt was trying to come through. Sid had told her that a woman in a wheelchair was coming through, but at the time, it did not make sense to her. She later realized that her favorite aunt was in a wheelchair towards the end of her life. She also had a wonderful ADC where *somebody* led her to a sealed plastic container of family photographs in her garage that she thought were lost in Katrina. That is how it works. Once we open up, whether through using a medium or not, many messages can come through.

Chapter Twenty-Two
Healing From Grief

"For those who seek to understand it, death is a highly creative force. The highest spiritual values of life can originate from the thought and study of death." ~ Elisabeth Kubler-Ross

You will never stop grieving for your loved one. Grief is the price we pay for loving so intensely. That love continues on beyond this physical world. It is possible to continue to miss your loved one, while at the same time, treasuring and honoring their life. Keeping the memory of your loved one alive and allowing that memory to live through you is an attainable goal.

Remember, the best remedy for grief is to talk about your feelings. It is important to find a group or groups that make you feel safe and comfortable. Sometimes, especially when the loss is a child, it may be necessary to seek one-on-one counseling with a grief therapist. You will never get over missing your loved one. You will always have moments of sadness. You may flow back and forth in the various stages of grief for a very long time.

One thing that is best avoided is numbing your emotions with drugs or alcohol. When emotions, especially very intense sadness and anger are not released, they store in the body, only to emerge later in ways that make no sense. Many people use alcohol to anesthetize their feelings, but fail to realize that it is a depressant and actually worsens the situation. The same goes for recreational drugs.

If the loss is a child, know that you will never be the same person you were before you lost your child. But you can heal from the intense pain of your loss. You can learn ways to give a purpose to the love you feel for your child. Your love will live on. The memory of your child will, too.

Regardless of the loss, you can move from pain to acceptance, and find solace somewhere in between. Acceptance isn't saying that you like it or you are happy with it; it just means *it is*. By healing and finding acceptance, you can remember the love and the happiness you shared with your loved one while he/she was here with you.

I am who I am today because I had Stephanie in my life. Every decision I made for thirty years was made with her in mind, first and foremost. When Stephanie died, my dear friend and publisher, Allan Gilbreath came to be a pall bearer for her, and give emotional support. Allan told me of a beautiful Chinese tradition. When loved ones pass away, each guest at the funeral is given a coin and a piece of hard candy. He explained that it represented the knowledge that that person made one's life richer and sweeter. My life is definitely richer and sweeter because Stephanie was my child. I will always love and miss her. It is because she is so loved that the emptiness I feel in her loss is so vast. I remind myself every day how fortunate I was to have her in my life and for as long as I did. She was a gift and a blessing.

Everyone who met Stephanie felt richer and sweeter because of it. She possessed a radiance that most regular people do not. Anyone who was exposed to her joy couldn't help but walk away feeling better. She had that effect on everyone she met.

It is very important to keep the memory of our loved ones alive. We want others to remember our loved ones. We want to talk about their lives. We want to hear their names spoken. One of the biggest mistakes people can make when someone loses a loved one is to avoid talking about that person; especially if it's a child. Many people are uncomfortable with death and do not know what to say to the bereaved. No one should ever have to apologize to anyone for feeling the way they do if they are grieving the loss of a loved one. When someone loses a loved one, it is important to that person to create memorials for the lost love. Even after they have left this physical world, our loved ones are still very much a part of our lives. As long as we live, their memory is kept alive.

One of the most beautiful memorials was a book that my friend Tanya put together. It documented different memories that various people shared about Stephanie. It meant the world to me that she thought enough of Stephanie to remember her in such a beautiful tribute. Someone else took song lyrics and added her photograph, which turned into flyers, given out at her funeral. These mementoes are priceless to us. They are our only connection to our loved one.

In the memorial book, Allan Gilbreath wrote:

My favorite memory of Stephanie is from a Saturday night at a convention. She was looking even more upbeat than usual. What I did not know was that one of the ballrooms was being cleared for a costume rave and she knew it.

When the music started, Stephanie armed with glow sticks and strips began her boogie. She danced without a care in the world. She wasn't trying to impress anyone or get anyone's attention. She danced for the pure joy of dancing. Stephanie danced the perfect dance. I don't think I will ever see such pure joy like that again.

What Allan did not see was the pure joy in my heart as I watched her enjoy herself. Nothing made me happier than to see her be happy.

She always had a way of touching people without even trying. During a film shoot in Mississippi, we filmed at one of the actor's home. There was a small yard with a doghouse where one of the family's dogs had a litter of puppies. Stephanie had never seen a nest of puppies or any other animal. She went into the yard and sat for hours watching the tiny pups crawl about inside the doghouse.

Jennifer, the owner, wrote of this moment in the memorial book:

Kalila Smith with Stephanie Link

She spent hours playing with them. She was just full of awe and wonder, and it renewed my hope for mankind in one fell swoop. The beauty and innocence she represented made me feel honored to share that moment, and it's one I will cherish for my entire life.

Her step-father, Sidney, wrote in her obituary:

Stephanie loved life and embraced all it had to offer, while touching the lives of many. Her smile and laughter were radiant.

I embrace these memories and those that I have shared with her to give me solace. I will always miss her, but do find some peace in knowing that she had a beautiful life. I gave her the very best I could, despite the limitations.

More interactive ways to honor a memory is to release butterflies, balloons, or Chinese lanterns in a public place. You can invite friends and family and make an event of it; or keep it personal. There is no right or wrong way to honor someone's memory. Some people make a quilt or item from the loved one's clothing. Others decorate the gravesite or make memorial gardens in their yard. Most of us know what made that person happy, and we include those things in the garden. Stephanie loved butterflies, so I found some butterfly garden sticks online and added those to a garden. I had a brick made with her name and a garden stone as well. I also had some large rocks that she had at one time painted at summer camp and added those to make it even more personal to her.

Memorials can be as simple or elaborate you want it to be. The main thing is that it makes you feel better. We create objects or a place to go that helps us remember the love we shared with our loved ones. We can visit them when we want to feel close to them, when we want to talk to them, and when we want to remember those precious times we spent with them.

Our memories of our loved ones are what console us now. It is the love we still feel that heals us. Once, I was in full blown depression. I found every little task extremely difficult. All I wanted to do was sleep, but sleep was the one thing that eluded me. The stress I held in my body was unlike anything I had experienced before. Some days, I spent hours just staring at the computer at grief posts, while other days, I could not sit still. I felt agitated and exhausted all at once. Getting the lawn cut, washing a load of clothes, or cleaning the kitchen became major undertakings. It is important to listen to your body during grief. If you feel like crying, then cry. If you can afford it, take some time off from work and relax. If you feel tired, get extra sleep. One of the most difficult things for me but most therapeutic was to find something, anything to laugh at every day.

It is hard to laugh or feel good during grief. It is essential, however, to take breaks from intense grieving and one way is to laugh. One of my daughter's most memorable qualities was the way she could make people laugh and smile. Everyone who ever came in contact with her walked away, not just feeling good, but laughing. One couldn't help but feel good around her. She loved to laugh, and took great pride in making others laugh with her. Laughter is truly one of the best medicines. Every night when I had my good cry, I would follow it by watching something funny on television. Those few moments of lightening the mood were very healing for me. Our bodies cannot handle being in extreme stress twenty-four hours a day. It would be extremely detrimental to our physical and mental health. We have to take a break from the pain, even if it's just for a half of an hour at a time. It is important to give the nervous system a rest from the intense stress of grieving. It is also equally important to not feel guilty for feeling good for a moment, or laughing at something that we find funny. Fortunately, I knew that as much as laughter played an important part of my daughter's life, she would want me to find humor in life. I don't believe that any of our deceased loved ones would want us to spend our lives in constant pain and suffering; no more than we would want that for them if we had left them behind.

Another great way to counteract the physical effects of grief and stress is to exercise. One of the most difficult things to do when we are in the throngs of intense grief is to get our bodies moving. I often felt frozen, as if I were in suspended animation. Unfortunately, due to this inactivity and emotional eating, I have put on a great deal of weight in a very short amount of time. I needed to get moving.

Another great outlet for depression is yoga and meditation. Meditation, whether quiet, seated or meditation in motion as with yoga or tai chi, gives the nervous system a break from stress. The purpose of any kind of meditation is to reach a state where the mind is turned off and the focus is in the now. Even a few minutes of this break is a great respite and beneficial for the body, mind, and spirit.

Focusing on breathing can keep the mind from drifting, therefore cutting off that continual barrage of inner dialogue and racing thoughts. Meditation can lower blood pressure and heart rate, reduce and eventually stop the over release of stress hormones, and promote feelings of well-being and peace. Another great way to achieve this is through massage therapy. It can calm nervous system and prevent stress from building up in the muscles causing pain and risking injury. Recent studies who that coloring produces the same effect on the mind and body as does meditation.

Writing is an excellent way to disburse and work through emotional roller coaster of grief. I started a grief journal writing to Stephanie to work out my inner conflict. I wrote to her as if I was having a conversation with her. Some days I wrote nothing, other days I couldn't stop writing. Some days I wrote of shock and confusion. Some days I wrote of guilt, apologizing for not being able to save her from death. I wrote how much I loved and missed her. The purpose is to prevent holding the emotions inside. Repressed emotions will store in the body causing pain, risk of injury, and even disease. Releasing the emotions through writing and reading back what is written is extremely powerful and therapeutic.

Besides writing this book and another, the other thing that eased my grief was my obsession with finding ways to communicate with Stephanie. Many people thought I was out of my mind, but the more I learned about NDEs, ADCs, and death bed visions, the more convinced I became that life truly continued beyond this one. The more belief I had in an afterlife, the less I suffered. I had more hope that I would be reunited with my daughter and other loved ones. I became convinced that she not only still existed somewhere, but she was not alone. She was in a wonderful place and with others who loved and cared for her. This gave me great comfort. The more I felt comforted, the more signs I continued to receive. With each new sign, my new relationship with my daughter strengthened and the bond between us grew.

Chapter Twenty-Three
Living Life in a New Way

"How long you grieved, does not reflect how much you loved." ~ Dr. Phil

Why must we wait for the death of someone we love or a near death experience of our own to begin really living? Most of us get comfortable in our lives and daily routines become mundane. We get caught up in work or other activities and we lose sight of what is important. We fall into the mindset that we will live forever. Then when someone close to us dies unexpectedly we are blindsided with grief wishing we would have had more time.

One of the things I was very happy about is that I took my daughter on several trips in the year before her untimely death. She attended a summer camp every year in Florida so she always had a summer vacation. I sometimes drove her so that she could also enjoy a visit to the beach. In the summer of 2011, we made a major trip out of it by bringing my granddaughters along and visited Busch Gardens in Tampa. It had been many years since we had spent time at a large amusement park although we had visited the ones in Orlando many times. I always tried to keep vacations unique. We had never been to Busch Gardens. On the drive home, we spent a day at one of the beaches to top it all off. It was already difficult for Stephanie to walk long distances at this point. She spent most of the trip in a wheelchair.

One of the things she wanted to do most of all was ride the big roller coaster. I have never been a fan of roller coasters. In fact, I am terrified of heights. I did not like any of the kids on those things; I especially did not want Stephanie to ride. On this trip she begged me to ride on one of the largest, fastest roller coasters in the park, The Sand Serpent. At first I objected, but after much begging, I reluctantly said, "Okay."

She was on cloud nine! She waited in line with such anticipation as if it was the happiest moment of her life. For all I know, it might have been. She was twenty-eight and I had never allowed her to get on a ride like that. She and all three of her nieces climbed into the monstrous ride. I stood on the sidelines with knots in my stomach. I positioned myself with the video camcorder to record the event. I watched in horror as this thing raced around the elevated track at high speed catching every breathtaking moment on video. After they finished the ride, we purchased the photograph that the park takes as they drop from the highest point on the track.

The five by seven photograph showed three teenage girls holding onto the safety bar, screaming at the top of their lungs in terror. The middle one, Megan shut her eyes tightly; her head facing down. Stephanie on the other hand who had never ridden a large roller coaster in her life was holding onto the bar, looking straight forward; laughing hysterically. The look on her face is absolute exhilaration. She was completely fearless. Even though it was one of my most nervous moments of letting go and allowing her to experience it, for her, it was one of the most joyous moments of her life. I am so glad that I videotaped it and purchased that photograph. It is priceless.

Five months later, Stephanie accompanied me on another Florida trip. This time we visited Key West. I was in the process of rewriting *Miami's Dark Tales* and wanted to add the Key West stories but needed to make it complete by including an actual visit. We flew into Miami and rented a car and made the long drive down to the keys. She followed along to some of the most interesting places: the Hemingway house where she saw the six-toed cats, the East Martello Museum where she saw Robert, the haunted doll, and hurricane grotto of Our Lady of Lourdes. She ate a Cuban sandwich on Duval Street and cooled off with a soft drink in one of Hemingway's famous haunts. The photos I took on this trip are now part of my treasured memories of her.

Afterlife Mysteries Revealed

From January 2012 through early January 2013, Stephanie made two trips to Memphis. On the first, she fulfilled her long time wish to see Graceland. She danced at a rave with glow sticks at a sci-fi conference and ate barbeque on Beale Street. During that same time frame she made several trips to Mississippi while filming a werewolf movie. She also spent a long weekend in Hollywood visiting friends and checking out Universal Studios.

During the filming of *Curse of the Rougarou*, a micro-budget werewolf movie that I wrote and filmed in a small rural town in Mississippi, she decided that she wanted to be in the movie. She had appeared before in various productions, one of which was *Journey into Darkness...The Trilogy*, a documentary that is sold on the tours. She watched scene after scene with actors being "killed" by the werewolf. She and I were staying in cabin in a state forest nearby the shoot location.

One evening, I noticed her in the bathroom in front of the mirror. And I heard her say, "...that wasn't good, do it again. Ok, now, die."

I asked what she was doing and she told me that she had a question for me. I asked her what was the question and she then asked if I could cast her in the movie to also be killed by the rougarou. At first I told her no. But like the roller coaster episode, she begged and pleaded and even "auditioned." She showed me how she had been practicing getting killed and that she could "get it right." I could not refuse her. I immediately rewrote a scene giving her a role. One of the perks of being writer and director is being able to change a script on a whim. Stephanie rehearsed all evening for her "big scene" the next day.

Stephanie was elated during the entire shoot. After her scene was shot, she watched it again and again. She was so proud of herself. I edited the scene later in post and she had a chance to see it a few times. When she died, the first thing I thought of was how I would never be able to look at that scene. Here she was dead, and the final shot was of her dead on the floor in a pool of fake blood. How could I possibly ever look at that?

Kalila Smith with Stephanie Link

I discussed the situation with my publisher and co-writer/executive producer, Allan Gilbreath and with my ex-husband who had also appeared in the production. They both agreed that I could not remove her kill scene from the movie. This was an important moment for her and she would want the film to be completed exactly the way it was, with her being killed by a rougarou. I realized that they were right. This was part of my precious memories with her. This scene in particular was a very special moment for her and something that she would most definitely want completed. I had to deal with it and I'm glad I did. Again, regardless of what I felt, this was not about me, it was *her* precious moment. Now that she is no longer here it is my precious memory. I can now smile when I think of that scene and how we got there.

One of the things my therapist had me complete was a list of all of the things I had learned from my daughter. The first thing, of course, was love. She loved everyone and everything unconditionally. She was pure love personified. If ever anyone was an angel in a human body, it was Stephanie. Everyone who came in contact with her walked away feeling good, smiling, and knowing that being in her presence was a special experience. One of Stephanie's gifts was to accept everyone and everything "as is."

I also learned not to judge. She met people at their level. She judged only based on how they treated her. She also taught me to be more forgiving. She never held grudges even though she certainly had boundaries and would get angry if people treated her unfairly. She had a great love and appreciation for nature and animals. As exemplified by the roller coaster episode, she was fearless. She lived in the moment. She enjoyed and appreciated whatever she was doing to its fullest, whether it was a meal or a video game. She made the most of every moment. She was the best teacher on gratitude. She appreciated everything she had and was able to do.

Given the fact that she had a severe disability, she never focused on it. For a person with Down syndrome, she was high functioning but still had major limitations both mentally and physically. She was very much aware of her limitations but never focused on what she could not do, just what she could. She embraced life with a passion that few of us regular people ever do. She had endless self-love and self-respect without being selfish or self-centered. We could all take lessons on how to live from Stephanie.

As mentioned before and in numerous resources, those who have experienced a NDE return to this life with a greater appreciation for life. Stephanie did not need a NDE to bring her to that state of awareness. Why wait for that anyway? What if we lived life to its fullest without having a NDE or the loss of someone we love? I find that even though I have not experienced any kind of NDE, the loss of my daughter made me realize how my priorities are where I really would want them. How grateful I am that I took the time to spend with her; including her in my projects and daily routines, and taking trips with her. I am very thankful that I had the gift of this very special person as my daughter for almost thirty years. I am most grateful that I can look back and say that my only regret was that she left too soon. I do know that I did to the very best of my ability treasure the time I had with her and made the most of every moment.

Not only has my perspective of life changed but also of death. Since my daughter's death, I look at death from a more realistic perspective. I no longer fear death. I no longer considered it *the end*. When my friend Betty died, I felt much more at peace than I ever had when I've lost people who were close to me. When another close friend died in January 2012, also from cancer in her seventies, my reaction was very different. She had been a long time teacher and mentor in therapeutic circles. I managed to not only completely avoid seeing her sick, but somehow managed to be out of town for her services. I avoided and denied her death so I didn't have to deal with it. It was not until my daughter died and I faced my grief head on that I was able to accept my avoidance of others' deaths.

It was too uncomfortable for me. Rather than show respect and mourn the loss, I hid and pushed it aside. When Gary died seven months after my teacher, there was no place to hide. I had to face the loss. Two months later, I pushed him and his music onto a back burner and hid in my work once again. When my daughter died, I could not push the loss of my child away. As ugly as it was, I had to face my grief.

The confirmations that I have received over and over from my daughter serve to prove that she still exists. She is somewhere else, and much closer than I had ever imagined. She hears me, she feels me; she is with me. It is this knowledge that saved me from drowning in despair and depression. I know that not only can I still be close to her, although not as I preferred, I will also someday reunite with her and my other loved ones.

My ability to communicate back and forth with her from the other side is the only thing that keeps me together. It has changed my outlook on life and death.

Many of my questions are still unanswered and for certain my quest for more knowledge will continue beyond this book. My views as well as my priorities have changed. Although I still miss my daughter very much and continue to have bouts of severe grief, I try to appreciate what I have left in life. Like she did, I shall strive to focus on what I have rather than have not.

Learning the lessons from those who have experienced NDEs would serve to help all of us enjoy what time we have with our loved ones here. No one should ever have to look back on their life with regret. I read somewhere once that we usually do not regret what we did, but rather what we did not do. No one ever said, "I did too much. I loved too much. I risked too much."

As I walked through a grocery store today, down the baking goods aisle, I heard my daughter's voice in my head whispering, "Mom...marshmallows!"

Before I could assimilate that word in my thoughts my nose delighted in the sweet aroma of marshmallows. I have walked down aisles where there have been marshmallows many times before. Never did I notice the aroma that permeated through the plastic bags. It was not just the scent but also sight, my mind saw pink. Not necessarily any form, just pink fluffy cloud-like matter that had no specific shape or form it. Suddenly I realized that she was showing me marshmallows from her perspective. Perhaps she was so in tune in her life that when she walked down that same aisle this is what she experienced. Or maybe it is how it was perceived to her now on the other side. I do not know. That bit of information was not revealed to me. At the time it mattered not. The point was that I noticed something very subtle and that no one else might have noticed. There were others in the aisle; no one was making a big deal over the sweet aroma of marshmallows.

When I get messages from her or any other spirit for that matter, I refrain from analyzing it. That would be missing the point. The point is experiencing in the now. Enjoying the sensation merely for what it is. At that point in time, the sensation was the smell of marshmallows. Nothing else mattered, THAT *is* the point. That *is* living in the now. It was a short lived moment in time that I made a connection with my daughter on the other side and we shared an experience of smelling marshmallows. When she puts a thought in my head, it is lightning fast with no time to think or analyze it.

There are many lessons that we can learn from those on the other side. As I worked on this chapter, a stream of lessons popped into my head (courtesy of my daughter) faster than I could type:

>1. Live in the now. We have no guarantee of a tomorrow. The past is gone. Now is the only time we have for sure.
>
>2. Do not waste precious time on anger. You never know when that person you might be angry with is going to leave this life. Treat your children and other loved one as if you may never see them again. You never know when that might be true.
>
>3. Learn to forgive yourself and others.
>
>4. Do not play the blame game. Many things in life are unfair and we do not know why. I certainly do not know why my child was handicapped then died at a young age. Blaming yourself, others, or God does not bring your loved one back. It solves nothing. This is a

difficult lesson to learn but releasing anger and blame is a big step in healing grief.

    5. Do not get caught up in the insanity of over achieving. Accept who you are, what you are. Be happy with what you have now.

    6. Enjoy peaceful times.

    7. Soak up nature. Appreciate the sunset, the dazzling flowers, and the flight of a dragonfly. Take time to stop and smell the marshmallows.

She tells me, "Know that I am here, and know that you will be with me again."

Chapter Twenty-Four
Final Thoughts

"Love transcends death." Dr. Raymond Moody, MD, PhD

All of the evidence points in favor of the existence of an afterlife. Regardless if the information is coming from a minister or priest, a medical professional, a grief therapist, or a medium, the message is always the same. There is a life after death. We do get signs and messages from the other side. Many people who study and teach about the afterlife come along because of their own experiences with either near death or losing someone they love. Not only do we know at this point that our loved ones do exist on the other side but we also know that everyone crosses over when it is "their time." We have a purpose. We continue on in another life closer to a loving God.

Even though it's comforting to know that my daughter is somewhere safe, beautiful, and she is not alone, I still miss her. I still cry every day, but the difference is I now have hope that I will see her again. If she really is free and in a better place; happy and comfortable with no pain, I can find some solace that she did not have to suffer with what she faced.

When I asked Hugh Palmer if he really believed after what he had experienced with his father, he told me, "I think that it is real. I know it. I came from a skeptical background but the experience I had was tangible although hard to articulate. I believe that they contact us as best they can under the circumstances, including the limitations of our embodied nature and preconceptions and their constraints too."

Finding evidence that there is an afterlife has brought me a great deal of peace and comfort, which has brought me from the depths of agonizing grief to a more peaceful state. Not a day goes by that I do not wish things would have been different and she was still here. Nothing will make up for that. But knowing she waits for me on the other side allows me to stop focusing on the pain of the loss and celebrate her life. I thank God for giving me the gift that was my child's life. I am grateful for having her as long as I did and for the many memories I have of her life.

My friend, Phillip told me that the first step in gaining faith is admitting that you don't know that you have it. It puts you on the journey to learning true faith, not what you've read but what you know to be true.

Although I did not go through a NDE myself, through the death of my daughter I have gained more faith than I ever had. As she instructed, I plan to move forward in my spiritual growth and look forward to the day when I can see my daughter and other people that I loved one day. It has also given me a greater understanding of God and the sacredness of life and death.

I have also through my experiences and in writing this book embraced a new concept of death. I am no longer afraid to die. I no longer view death as an end.

I am forever changed by my loss but realize that I can never get my old life back. I have only two choices: the first is to become bitter and broken; forever looking back at the loss. The other is to continue to love this child as I did; honor her memory and continue on until it is my time to go. The first option is the easiest. Getting lost in our grief is effortless. I try to the best of my ability to accomplish the latter. Sometimes I fare well and some days I fail miserably at it. The emotional surges of grief are unpredictable. I can only strive to focus on the good memories. It is a bittersweet line to walk.

Nothing can ever replace the love and joy that she brought into my life. Stephanie brought happiness and laughter that I would not otherwise have experienced. I am who I am today because of the life I shared with her.

I will honor her wish and let go moving forward. I can release the pain, and still keep the memories. I can move forward from the loss and still continue to love and honor her memory. I can remember the good times we shared, and remember the love I felt for this very special child that I was so fortunate to have as my own.

It is my hope that sharing my journey will help others in their quests to prove that an afterlife exists. Knowing there is hope of reuniting on the other side can help heal your grief. You will still feel the pain, still miss the one you love, but hopefully the pain is softened by the knowledge that you will see them again. Hope is renewed; faith is restored; there is a promise of another world beyond this one.

For those who were skeptical or cynical, I hope that your mind has been opened to accept other possibilities exist. Perhaps this book will inspire you to delve further into knowing more about the afterlife.

If you are a family member of someone who is facing death, my hope is that you are comforted that your loved one will not go very far from you. I pray that you have the strength to stand next to that person through the end of their life, and give them the love and support they need and deserve when they leave this world.

For those who are facing death. Hopefully my own experiences will serve to give you comfort in your end days that you may relax and enjoy what is left without fear of what lies on the other side; knowing that someone dear will come for you, when it is your time to cross over. If nothing else has been proven, we know without a doubt that love never dies and we never die alone. It is love that connects us throughout our lives and into the next one.

Life is a gift from God. It gives us the opportunity to grow and get closer to Him. We take comfort in knowing that whatever pain or problems our loved ones had in this life do not follow them in the life hereafter. We are given the gift of signs from those who have crossed over. They reassure us and encourage us to continue on and to be happy. Always the message is to love.

Today I begin a new journey stepping forward to grow spiritually. I step forward to push myself to my limits; to pick up where I left off many years ago when I finished my education.

Kalila Smith with Stephanie Link

Once again, I set out to find out who I am, this time. All the while, I keep in my heart the memories of my daughter and the many years that I spent caring for her.

Resources

Near Death Experience Research Foundation (NDERF) Dr. Jeffrey and Jody Long www.nderf.org

After Death Communication Research Foundation (ADCRF) Dr. Jeffrey and Jody Long www.adcrf.org

The Compassionate Friends - www.compassionatefriends.org

Dr. Raymond Moody - raymondmoody.org/ www.lifeafterlife.com/

Eternea – where science meets spirituality www.eternea.org

Medium Sid Patrick – www.sid-patrick.com

ADC's Bill & Judy Guggenheim - www.after-death.com

Kalila Smith personal page - www.kalilasmith.com

https://www.facebook.com/AfterlifeMysteriesRevealed

Bibliography and Suggested Reading

Bozarth, Ph.D, Alla Reneé, *A Journey Through Grief: Gentle, Specific Help to Get You Through The Most Difficult Stages of Grief,* Philadelphia, Hazelden 1994, Print

Duminiak, Christine, *Heaven Talks To Children: Afterlife Contacts, Spiritual Gifts, and Loving Messages,* New York, Citadel Press, 2010, Print

----

God's Gift Of Love: After-Death Communications: For Those Who Grieve, Create Space, 2003, Print

Parisien, Ara, *The Other Side of Grief,* self-published, 2010, Print

Sanders, Dr. Catherine M, *Surviving Grief,* New Jersey, Wiley, 1992, Print

----

How to Survive the Loss of a Child, New York, Three Rivers Press, 1998, Print

McVea, Crystal, *Waking up in Heaven,* Tennessee, Howard Books, 2013, Print

Jung, Carl, *Memories, Dreams, Reflections,* U.K., Gardners Books, 1995, Print

Pisegna, Father Cedric, *Death, The Final Surrender,* California, 2012, Print

Guggenheim, Bill and Judy, *Hello from Heaven,* New York, Bantum Books, 1995, Print

Woerlee, Gerald, *Mortal Minds: A Biology of the Soul and the Dying Experience,* New York, Prometheus Books, 2003, Print

Eadie, Betty, *Embraced by the Light,* New York, Bantum Books, 1992, Print

Moody, Dr. Raymond A., *Life After Life*, New York, Bantum Books, 1975, Print

Moody, Dr. Raymond A., and Paul Perry, *Reunions: Visionary Encounters With Departed Loved Ones*, Vermont, Ballantine Books, 1993, Print

----

Glimpses of Eternity, New York, Guideposts, 2010, Print

"When Loved Ones Die," DVD

Perry, Paul, *Afterlife*, Documentary, Vanguard Cinema, 2007, DVD,

Schwartz, PhD, Gary, *The G.O.D. Experiments*, New York, Atria Books, 2007, Print

----

The Sacred Promise, New York, Atria Books, 2011, Print

The Afterlife Experiments, New York, Atria Books, 2001, Print

Long, Dr. Jeffrey, *Evidence of the Afterlife*, New York, Harper Collins, 2010, Print

Lumpkin, Joseph, *Fallen Angels, the Watchers, and the Origins of Evil*, Alabama, Fifth Estate, 2006, Print

Leonardi, Lillie, *In the Shadow of a Badge: A Memoir about Flight 93, a Field of Angels, and My Spiritual Homecoming*, New York, Hay House 2013, Print

Willis-Brandon, Carla, *One Last Hug Before I Go*, Florida, Health Communication, Inc. 2000, Print

----

Heavenly Hugs, New Jersey, Career Press, 2013, Print

Kagan, Annie, *The Afterlife of Billy Fingers: How My Bad-Boy Brother Proved to Me There's Life After Death*, Virginia, Hampton Roads Press, 2013, Print

Kubler-Ross, Dr. Elisabeth, and David Kessler, *On Grief and Grieving*, Print

Kübler-Ross, Dr. Elisabeth, *On Life After Death*, Print

Daniel, Terri, *A Swan in Heaven: Conversations Between Two Worlds*, Oregon, First House Press, 2008, Print

----

Embracing Death: A New Look at Grief, Gratitude, and God, Oregon, National Book Network, 2010, Print

Article, Daily News, *Oklahoma woman shares her near-death experience of dying and talking with God for nine minutes,* April 3, 2013, Print

Article, *Near-Death Experiences More Vivid Than Real Life,* Real Science, Tia Ghose, April 5, 2013, Print

Article, *Afterlife feels even more real than real,* researcher says. Ben Brumfield, CNN, April 10, 2013, Print

Article, *Dialogue with the dead is feasible, Vatican spokesman says,* John Hooper, London Observer Service, January 1, 1999, Print

Article, *Mystery surrounds tragic accident; Friend thinks woman killed in crash made phone call before dying,* Miami Sun-Sentinel by Donna Pazdera, March 3, 1998, Print

Paul McCartney *After Death Communication* Article, Infobeat, May 1, 2001, Print

Famous After Death Communications, Article, Asbury Park Press, Associated Press, October 1996, Print

Article, *Former FBI Agent Recalls seeing Angels at 9/11 Crash Site,* Michael Ireland Senior International Correspondent, ASSIST News Service, June 6, 2012, Print

Article, USA Weekend, *Michael Jordan After Death Communication,* Kathleen McCleary, November 15, 1996, Print

Article, *The Near-Death Experience,* David Ritchie, June 4, 2013, Print

Article, *Do loved ones bid farewell from beyond the grave?* John Blake, CNN, September, 2011, Print

Article, *Is Hell Real?* David Sessions, Feb 8, 2013, Print

Article, *Between the material and the supernatural: Therapeutic implications of bereaved individuals' experience of contact with the deceased person,* Hugh Palmer, 2009, Print

Article, *Afterlife Awareness Conference coming to St. Louis,* The Edge Magazine, 2013

About the Author

Kalila Smith is a Certified Gestalt Therapist and NLP Practitioner who spent her entire life experiencing visits from spirits. For over two decades she investigated and wrote about paranormal research and communication with spirits. But in January 2013 all that she believed was shattered when her youngest daughter died unexpectedly. Her entire world was turned upside down and her belief system challenged as she worked through the grief of losing her child and embarked on a spiritual journey to find her on the other side.

Stephanie Link was twenty-nine years old when she died suddenly from a rapid spreading antibiotic-resistant infection following a tonsillectomy. Born with Down syndrome, she spent her entire life being cared for by her mother. Although Stephanie had extreme limitations due to her medical condition, she had a strange connection to the spirit world throughout her entire life. Now, she continues to walk in both worlds, sending messages to her mother from the Other Side.

Kalila's other books include:
New Orleans Ghosts
Voodoo, & Vampires
Tales from the French Quarter
Miami's Dark Tales
Searching for Spirits: The Ultimate Guide for Ghost Hunters
Séance Experiments

Discover other fine publications at:

http://www.darkoakpress.com

www.ingramcontent.com/pod-product-compliance
Lightning Source LLC
LaVergne TN
LVHW011417080426
835512LV00005B/109